W9-BXT-741

ESSAYS IN ORDER : 4

THE BOW IN THE CLOUDS

THE MACMILLAN COMPANY
NEW YORK · BOSTON · CHICAGO · DALLAS
ATLANTA · SAN FRANCISCO

THE BOW IN THE CLOUDS.

*An Essay towards the Integration
of Experience*

BY

E. I. WATKIN

ἴρισσιν ἐοικότες, ἅς τε Κρονίων
ἐν νέφεϊ στήριξε, τέρας μερόπων ἀνθρώπων.
Iliad Λ 27.

*Dixitque Deus: Hoc signum foederis quod do inter me et
vos, et ad omnem animam viventem, quae est vobiscum in
generationes sempiternas: Arcum meum ponam in nubibus,
et erit signum foederis inter me et inter terram.*
GENESIS IX. 12, 13.

NEW YORK
THE MACMILLAN COMPANY
1932

COPYRIGHT, 1932,
BY THE MACMILLAN COMPANY.

All rights reserved—no part of this book may be
reproduced in any form without permission in writing
from the publisher, except by a reviewer who wishes
to quote brief passages in connection with a review
written for inclusion in magazine or newspaper.

Set up and printed.   Published February, 1932.

BT
135
.W28
1932

SET UP BY BROWN BROTHERS LINOTYPERS
PRINTED IN THE UNITED STATES OF AMERICA
BY THE FERRIS PRINTING COMPANY

CANISIUS COLLEGE LIBRARY
BUFFALO, N. Y.

CONTENTS

FOREWORD ·

THE following essay makes no claim to be a scientific elaboration of its thesis, the affirmation of the metaphysical order of reality as revealed in the varieties of human experience and the integration of human experience by that order. Its more modest scope is but to contemplate that order of experience from various points of view and different levels in the hope that the view from one point may supplement and illuminate the view from another, until the reader catches a glimpse of the mountain of being as it rises from the impenetrable darkness of matter to the impenetrable light of God. If therefore the treatment of my theme appear too loose and discursive, so that I may be thought to have used the rainbow, as St. Bridget is related to have employed a sunbeam, as my clothes-line, the clothes in this instance being thoughts long pondered and long cherished on various more or less cognate subjects, be this my justification. To acknowledge all my debts would be impossible. But I would take this opportunity to point out that the extent of my obligation to Dr. Peter Wust, Mr. Christopher Dawson and Professor Lossky far exceeds what the references to their work would suggest.

E. I. W.

October 2nd, 1931.

SYNOPSIS

and real factors. Significance and prospects of Bolshevism and Fascism. (*d*) *History* reveals the interplay of ideal and real factors.

BLUE: METAPHYSICS

Metaphysics founded upon intellectual intuition. Nature and scope of intuition. Intuition, (1) abstract and distinct, (2) concrete and obscure. Ultimates shown 'monstrated' to intuition. Example, the metaphysical proofs of theism. The 'contemplative method' its nature and necessity. Ultimate facts of experience inexplicable by their conditions or concomitants. Metaphysics indispensable and universal. Popular and scientific metaphysics. Modern rejection of metaphysics. Mental phenomena more real than physical. No organic culture possible without a metaphysical foundation. The range of metaphysics. Metaphysical contemplation of God in the ideas. Deductive teleological science impossible. Mysticism the supernatural crown of metaphysics.

GREEN: LIFE

Concrete union with biological life outside and within man. Nature polytheism the worship of natural life and energy. Primitive monotheism obscured. Christianity and biological life: respect for the healthy body. The Holy Spirit Giver of natural life. The advance and unfolding of life a wedlock of matter-energy and form, the progressive information of matter and the substitution of intrinsic for external law. Evolution: phenomenal emergence, noumenal creation.

YELLOW: ART

Formal or ideal theory of art. Art presents the significant form imperfectly embodied in nature. Realism and expressionism. Human art and evolution. Artistic display of pattern. The historian as artist. Didactic art justified when the idea it expresses is its organic form. Individual art based upon a social art embodying the same significant form, an idea or system of ideas. Necessity of social art exemplified by the failure of the Gothic Revival. The artist's union with his object concrete and vital. Æsthetic intuition of pattern invested with the quality of beauty, the resplendence of form or pattern. The arts reflect and continue aspects of the Divine Art. Tragedy and religion. Art, a revelation of Divine Immanence, leads to the threshold of religion.

ORANGE: SEX

Sex the culmination of biological life and reflection of supernatural love. The modern sex cult. Sex and mystical religion.
Critique of the sexual explanation of religion. Likenesses between
sexual and religious experience. Vital energy the common substratum of both. The Saints not sex-frustrated. Sex the image of
religion, not *vice versâ*. The sex cult a disguised religious sup-
pression: D. H. Lawrence. The sacred marriage pagan and Christian. Romantic and modern attitudes to sex compared and criti-
cised. The biological not the spiritual. Spiritual love in God.

RED: RELIGION

Ecstatic peace the gift of religious experience. Religious experience not to be condemned for abuses and excesses. Direct and
distinctive experience of a religious object, value, quality, despite
a subjective factor, an intuition of objective reality, neither emotional nor irrational. Data of religious experience utilised and controlled by discursive reason. Individual experience insufficient.
The witness of Saints and public revelation. Institutional religion
indispensable. Religious experience the soul of religion: its body,
theology and cultus. Conceptual translation of religious experiences. Analysis of Pascal's Memorial. Concordant testimony of
saints and mystics. Christianity the most adequate presentation
and most complete harmony of religious truth. Transcendental
religion supernatural. The *mysterium tremendum* and *fascinosum*.
The immediate intuition of God: Père Picard. God revealed in
the Saints. The Communion of Saints, the soul of the Church.

ULTRA-RED: MYSTICISM

Mystical union the organic fulfilment of the life of grace.
Mystical experience consciousness of God's supernatural presence
and operation in the soul. High union not always conscious;
mystical union without its intuition. The centre of the soul the
seat of mystical union. Prejudice against mysticism due to mis-
conceptions of its nature. Mystical experience transcends images
and concepts. The negative theology.

CONCLUSION

Presence and operation of God at every level and in every form
of human experience. A comprehensive vision.

THE BOW IN THE CLOUDS

THE BOW IN THE CLOUDS

INTRODUCTORY

Ecce ponam arcum meum in nubibus—'Behold, I set my bow in the clouds.' Man's entire path lies among clouds. Never a day when his intellectual sky is clear and the sun visible. Only an ever-shifting cloudland—now dark with lowering storm clouds, now the breaking tempest, now a leaden expanse of dull monotony, now mist and driving rain, or again higher and whiter clouds, bright with the light of the sun they veil. But they never disperse, and if there is a passing rift it is night, and we see only stars. For our very essence is set between being and nonentity—the Absolute Being of God and its polar antithesis, the nothingness from which He drew us. A world of shadow and obscurity—the half-world of natural creation, where, by the intrinsic law of its deficiency, error is the invariable concomitant of truth, evil of good. And our knowledge is doubly limited—limited as the knowledge not only of a created, but further of an embodied, intelligence.

1

Reality, whatever its kind and level, reaches us doubly modified, by the inherent limits of our intellect and our large dependence on the senses. Clouds on every side. Below, the cloud of ultimate matter —the least degree of being. What is matter? We do not know. Or life? Another cloud. Closer still —our own nature. What is the soul? How is it united with the body? Clouds. And above us—God is hidden in the 'cloud of unknowing,' His infinite and incomprehensible transcendence.

This is not pessimism: the shadows of this half-world 'are of good things', and, in so far as they exist positively, are themselves good. And there is great beauty, ever-changing play of light and shade, shifting contours, subtle undertones of colour. But since we are spirits, we crave a sure knowledge of truth, a permanent satisfying good. Like the Lady of Shalott in her magic bondage, we would escape the prison-house of subjective experience—the shadows of shadows. Nor can any shadows, however lovely, still the soul's demand for reality. 'I am half sick of shadows.'

There is, however, a rainbow in the clouds of our ignorance, which refracts in the limited being of creatures the pure white light of the Divine Sun, too dazzling for mortal vision, into a spectrum of seven hues, themselves complex of an indefinite variety of minor shades. This bow of God is a pledge to man that the deluge—the chaos of formless or well-nigh formless energy—shall never engulf him and all his works. Creation, continued in the long evolution of creatures, has been a gradual triumph over that chaos, the watery abyss upon which the Creative Spirit has brooded from the beginning. And human achievement continues and completes that victory. This work shall never be undone: the creative development shall not be made void—still less its crown, man's life and work, intellectual and social —but fulfilled in a consummation of unguessed perfection. Such is the assurance of the rainbow—the reflection of God in the many levels and forms of human experience, and the reality it has revealed and shall reveal hereafter.

Symbolism, the reader may object—surely a *jeu démodé*—a quaint conceit of fancy, worked to death by the Fathers and mediæval exegetes—moreover quite arbitrary and fantastic in the extreme. No doubt symbolism may be, and has been, abused, as literal exegesis of Scripture or as supplying the premises of a demonstration. But to go to the other extreme, and reject all symbolism in our interpretation of God's written or unwritten Scripture, is to deny the analogy which everywhere obtains between the various levels of being, in virtue of which the lower is always representative of the higher—the extended physical shape, for example, an embodiment or external representation (as Wust has pointed out)[1] of an interior and immaterial form. 'All things' are thus 'double one against the other' —outer corresponding with inner, material with spiritual. To be blind to this inner significance is to refuse credit to the vision of the poet or artist. It is what Blake condemned as 'single vision.'

Since, however, the same physical object in its different aspects symbolises a multiplicity of spiritual realities, symbolism involves a factor of subjective and arbitrary choice. But this is true of art generally. Even science selects its data and angle of vision. It must also be admitted that of all forms of symbolism the symbolism of colour has perhaps been the most abused. Its devotees have lost sight of the necessary element of arbitrary selection, have forgotten that the same colour suggests a different significance to different minds and temperaments. Yet it cannot be wholly arbitrary. Despite the Chinese use of yellow for funerals, black as the absence of colour is definitely the analogue and therefore the embodi-

[1] *Die Dialektik des Geistes,* pp. 116, *seq.*

ment and symbol of mourning and loss. White, the perfect fullness of all colour, has an intrinsic affinity with the positive purity of integral being. Red, the hue of flame and life-blood, is the natural symbol of love, the flame and flower of life natural and supernatural. And for the rest symbolism is pre-eminently a method of statement, a presentment of truth to the imagination. Indeed, if it were nothing more than an imaginative *memoria technica,* it would be sufficiently justified.

For these reasons I have ventured to set out under the symbolism—admittedly to a large extent arbi-trary—of the colours of the rainbow some thoughts as to the forms by which God reveals Himself in human experience, as a guarantee of man's know-ledge and endeavour now, and the pledge, because the earnest, of a final manifestation which shall sat-isfy every need of his heart, perfecting his know-ledge and completing his achievement. The rainbow is the promise that the clouds will disperse and the sun shine from a clear sky.

To-day human knowledge and action are too often denounced as insignificant and illusory, if not indeed in their entire range—absolute scepticism is ex-tremely rare, and always theoretical—at least on some, usually the higher levels, and in particular our contacts with Absolute Reality. Man's personal unity and identity, his free and rational will, his religious experience, his spiritual and ethical ideals, his philosophy, are widely regarded as illusions, misinterpretations and perversions of purely biological facts, desires or instincts—the mere sum of activities and forces of a lower order. I am convinced that I am throughout my life myself. Surely a fact of primary self-evidence. No, protests Bertrand Russell, you are but a succession of atomic events, psychic or physical according to the aspect under which they are regarded. I believe I act thus or thus to serve God or help my fellows. No, reply the Behaviourists, your action is but an automatic nervous reflex which gave rise—how?—to the illusion of a rational motive. I believe myself able to control biological instinct in the service of a rational or spiritual end. No, it is commonly answered, you are but the tool of a blind and purely biological life-force, which, mocking you with the hallucination of its defeat, made you the instrument of its purpose.

To refute these partialities would exceed the limits of an essay. Moreover, we are concerned with ultimates. And of ultimates there is, and can be, no demonstration. We must employ what may be termed the contemplative method. That is to say, we must look at the fact, the datum of experience, as experienced by ourselves or recorded by reliable testimony,[2] and see what it is and what it involves.

For example, I look at the fact of my contingence, as I experience it, an ultimate fact of my being, and I see that it implies an absolute on which it depends for its existence and origin. I contemplate the ascending scale of perfection—physical energy, biological life, mind—and see that it implies perfect being at its summit. I experience an order in events and see that it implies a sufficient reason. No demonstrations, these, to the man who cannot see these implications himself and refuses to accept the word of others. But convincing none the less. Outside myself a web of ordered experience which is in large part simply given—often no agreeable gift. I see in it something not of my making, an objective reality. In such apperception I am not, I cannot be, a sceptic or pragmatist, nor even, when a physical obstacle defeats some rational purpose or requirement, an idealist. Always the same appeal to the *anima naturaliter sana*—the mind that is sound, that is 'whole'—to see what is shown to it. And the shower

---

[2] Some ultimates, of course, *e.g.* the objectivity of sense-data and the substantial unity of the self, can be established only from our personal experience. They are implied in the validity of all other witness.

is, in the last resort, God. Nor can His revelation be otherwise received. But many have never been shown certain truths and values—or, if at all, under false labels or in false light—and many have defective sight. Here lies the justification of a religious education—no imposition of ideas upon the unreceptive and recalcitrant, but simply the showing what is actually there and what otherwise they might not see. For not only are individuals intellectually or spiritually colour-blind or sufferers from astigmatism; entire groups, races or epochs display particular faults of vision, which require correction by reference to a complete body of truth handed down through the ages and taught universally.

As I set down under the imaginative symbolism of the spectrum—the colours of God's bow in the clouds—what I claim to be objective contacts with reality at its various levels, and in various modes, I ask my readers to interrogate impartially their own experience and the recorded experience of others. Is that experience justified, co-ordinated, harmonised and most adequately interpreted by accepting as objectively valid the forms of experience I have symbolised by these seven colours and those beyond violet and beyond red? I believe it is.

It should be pointed out that the scale of colours

does not wholly represent a progress in the order of being. The ascending scale of reality is crossed by another principle—the immediacy or mediacy of contact with the reality in question, as it is apprehended more concretely or more abstractly. Corresponding to that twofold movement of the Divine Life of which Ruysbroeck speaks [3] the going forth of the Persons and their return to the Unity of the Divine Nature—here, of course, inseparable aspects of the same act—is a dual movement throughout creation, as it were, the systole and diastole of the cosmic heart. There is a movement of immediate contact and union, and a complementary movement of distinction, a separation and holding apart. In man these two movements are represented respectively by concrete union with an external object or person, whether biological or metabiological,[4] that is spiritual; and the contemplation, as from a distance, of some aspect of a person or object.

Thus when a thirsty climber drinks from a mountain torrent his contact is of the former kind, immediate concrete union. When, his thirst quenched, he watches the beauty of the amber water as it swirls

---

[3] *Adornment of the Spiritual Marriage,* ii, chs. 48, 57, 63; iii, chs. 1, 3, 4.
[4] I employ a valuable term, coined, I believe, by Mr. Middleton Murry.

and breaks over the stones and throws back the light from gleaming pebble or edge of spray, his contact is more mediate and more abstract; it involves a certain separation from its object, being a contemplation of the beautiful colour and form of the stream abstracted from its concrete existence as this particular piece of water in its entirety. And still more abstract would be a study of the chemical properties of the water as stated in a work of science.[5] St. Augustine says of man that 'as spectator he is enlightened by God, as *participant* he is gladdened.' [6] This duality is true not only of his distinctively religious experience, but of his experience as a whole, which, however, is itself a contemplation or participation of God as reflected, expressed, and communicating Himself, in and by His Creatures. Man is everywhere a spectator, in the separative, indirect, and more abstract union of contemplation, or a participant, in the direct, concrete and contactual union.

It will, I think, be found that in some types of experience with which I shall deal—those symbolised by violet, indigo and blue—contemplative union

[5] The more concrete union is a union with the object as an actual substance compound of form and matter, the more abstract union a union with its form abstracted from the matter which gives it actual existence.

[6] *De Civ. Dei, XI*, xxiv, 41, quoted by Father Martin D'Arcy, S.J., in *A Monument to St. Augustine*, p. 168.

with the object predominates; in others—symbolised
by green, orange and red—the concrete and more
direct union predominates, physical, biological or
spiritual. The union of art, symbolised by yellow,
is intermediate, more concrete than the former, more
abstract than the latter.[7] In red, religious experience,
both types blend—though the latter is primary.

A reassertion of the metaphysical order of being as
experienced by man according to the dual mode of
contemplation and concrete union is the most urgent
need of the present day. On that order depends in
the last resort the entire order of human life, theoretical and practical, individual and social. The order
of being is the order of value, and the order of value
in turn the order of choice, of those loves which
determine human activity. 'He hath set love in order
within me.' The manifestation of this order is God's
bow of ascending reality and double reception. And
when modern speculation and literature are so preoccupied with the clouds of human experience—
unsolved problems of pain, wickedness and frustration, enigmas and blind alleys at the end of inquiries
where solution is impossible to human faculty, the

---

[7] For the union of art is not with the concrete object as such,
but with its form, but on the other hand with the form as embodied in the concrete and individual object. See further, pp. 99-
102, 106-109.

clash and contradiction of partial aspects professing themselves views of the whole, the groping of a bewildered agnosticism in the mist—it will not be amiss to point to this divine bow of truth spanning the vault of man's life and knowledge, to give him assurance that everywhere joy is truer, more real, more ultimate than pain, good than evil, and fulfilment than failure, that every problem has its solution, though at present but a hint, and that all apparent contradictions converge and are reconciled in the whole to which each partial aspect contributes and bears its witness.

God's bow, however, appears to Noah—man— only when with his three sons—Ham, sensation; Shem, intuition; Japheth, the discursive reason—he offers sacrifice to God: that is, when he directs himself in the humble worship of religion towards the Being from which his own being derives, and on which it depends, the Absolute Being, whose Name is Jahweh, I am who am. Religion alone can display God in His created expressions and images. And since the will is the function which directs the attitude of the soul, a right orientation of the will can alone turn the mind to this reflected vision of God. When the will does not direct its gaze the eye is blind. And in turn only God's grace can so direct and

fix the will that the mind beholds, spanning the vault
of being and experience, the seven-hued bow that
refracts His invisible light and tempers it to our mortal eye.

It is as to builders of a new human order that Jahweh displays this bow to Noah and his sons—pledge
that their work shall not be vain, and rule of its
structure. Man, by his co-operative labours in time
and space, must embody the order of God's reflection and self-donation in creatures, the metaphysical
order of being and value. He must erect on earth a
city of God, image and prophecy of the Jerusalem
which is above. And he must build into it every
form of positive experience; vertically from the
pleasures and apprehensions of sense to the supreme
contemplation of God; horizontally from the ordering of his own life as completely as his personal
vocation permits to the establishment of a social
order in which all vocations—forms of life and work
—have their place. The sanctuary for silent devotion,
the choir for liturgical praise, the university for philosophy and letters, the studio for art, the laboratory
for scientific research, the workshop for manufacture,
the market for commerce, landscape and garden for
the enjoyment of natural beauty, all must be there.
To its building the moralist must prescribe practical

rules for the order of individual life, the politician and economist for the order of society; the savant must observe and experiment, the philosopher behold the ideal principles of being and knowledge which the artist, poet, painter, sculptor, and craftsman must embody in forms of visible beauty; the athlete must express, through the development of his physical powers, the natural life they serve, and the lover unfold its flower. And above all these with supernatural love, the priest will worship, the contemplative enjoy, the God Who is first Cause and final End of all human activity.

To-day a flood of intellectual scepticism and social revolution has swept over the Western world. A building, venerable in its age but unsound, has been sapped, its foundations covered by the deluge. When the flood has completed the work for which it has been permitted, has demolished whatever in the edifice of past civilisation and belief is no longer solid, the eternal foundations on which it rested, and which many believe to have perished with the superstructure, will re-emerge, the evidence of their solidity more imposing than before. On them the builders of the future must erect a new order to the norm of the seven-hued bow whose bands rest on this substructure of human capacities and functions, being their fulfilment by God's self-revelation in the diverse forms of human experience. Meanwhile, it is our task to expose these foundations, the fundamental types of human function, to display the intrinsic and necessary order obtaining between them, to show how they receive objective reflections of the divine light between which a corresponding order subsists. As such they are the bases on which God's temple city must be rebuilt, more solidly and on a more comprehensive plan than before. To that reconstruction His rainbow is guide and promise.

ULTRA–VIOLET

MATTER

BELOW the first visible colour of the rainbow lie the ultra-violet rays—imperceptible to the eye, but of potent influence on the human body. Here we touch the last confines of being, where it trembles like a bubble on the verge of a dissolution, from which God's creative conservation withholds it, into the nothingness whence it was drawn. Nevertheless even this minimum of actual being is not sheer potency, the *materia prima*. A measure of form— an arrangement, or direction—renders actual the potential energy which is its substratum. The final secret of matter—by which I now mean the concrete matter of physical science—escapes the physicist's probing. And if we see in it energy informed by the order of its motion, rotation of negative electrons round a positive nucleus, or fluctuation of electron waves, this is but a blend of philosophic speculation with a physical hypothesis, perhaps as provisional as Ptolemaic—may we not add—Copernican astronomy. The economic mathematical symbolism which for the physicist has replaced the older atomic mechanism represents, and must of its nature represent, the 'form' of corporeal matter—not its 'matter', the potential energy, which cannot exist apart from the form which physics thus represents, and is therefore in itself essentially unknowable. Yet we may surely find with Faber [1] matter of religious contemplation in gazing down into these dark foundations of the universe, the almost chaotic sea of force on which architectonic Wisdom has erected the palace wherein she will receive those human guests in whose company she deigns to take her delight. *Deliciæ meæ cum filiis hominum.* Even here in the utmost depth there are images and analogies of the supreme height. The dance of the electrons around the proton is an image of the supernatural Communion of Saints wherein a countless host of spirits whose *separate* being is in a sense constituted by their need of God and receptivity of Him revolve like the negative electrons around the Absolute Positivity, the pole and centre of reality, eternally united, yet eternally distinct. Even the Blessed Trinity is shadowed by the mutual attrac-

[1] *The Blessed Sacrament,* p. 302.

tion of these infinitesimal particles of electric energy. And potential energy—the first matter—reflects the Father, the Source of the Divine Life; its form, the Son, the Logos; the actual energy which is the union of both, the Spirit of Divine Love proceeding from Father and Son conjointly.[2]

Material energy reflects on a lower plane the energy of the will—the former informed by the order of physical arrangement, the latter by the order of divine charity. Nowhere from the bottom to the summit of the ladder of being is there a complete break. Physical energy differs from biological instinct only by lack of being; it is biological instinct *minus*. Similarly, biological instinct differs from rational will by lack of being; it is will *minus*. And the concupiscent will of natural man is in turn a deficiency of being as compared with his will of supernatural love, receptive of the Absolute Will that is Love itself. Finally the obscurity, the enigma of matter, known only by its effects in so far as they can be formulated in mathematical sequence, but itself an unknown, indeed an unknowable, mirrors the transcendent incomprehensibility of God. And its

---

[2] St. Bonaventure puts forward a similar analogy. See Gilson, *Philosophie de S. Bonaventure,* p. 205.

operation, electric force, in itself also an unknown quantity, becomes manifest in the light and power it supplies. So the incomprehensible Godhead is revealed in the supernatural wisdom and love which He communicates to His Saints.

VIOLET

THE POSITIVE SCIENCES

VIOLET, the first visible colour of the rainbow, represents the knowledge of reality at its lower levels afforded by the physical and biological sciences, that is to say, man's more abstract knowledge of matter and biological life, and union with them—though it is a union which is also separation. All these sciences are based upon the abstraction and analysis by the discursive reason of appropriate data contained in the global intuitions of physical sensation. We cannot, it is true, draw a sharp line of demarcation between scientific abstraction and analysis and the unscientific experience which underlies and precedes formulated science. Only the most rudimentary sensations are pure intuitions of sense.[1] Such, for example, are the sense of light on first awakening from sleep, hearing a noise which might be anything from a thunderclap to the banging of a door, or the apprehension of water by a thirsty traveller. Normally our

[1] In all this I owe a great debt to the intuitionist epistemology of the Russian philosopher Lossky.

sense activities, however seemingly instantaneous, include a factor of rational analysis which selects from the complex of sensation significant forms, whereby the object perceived is related to others already known. It is at this point that error may supervene and give rise to false classifications and so-called hallucinations of sense. Thus the sciences do but continue in their more methodical procedure the rudimentary and careless 'science' of unmethodical experience.

Moreover the synthetic achievements of science—indeed the syntheses of ordinary experience—would be impossible without the intervention of a higher faculty or mode of operation, the intellectual intuition which directly apprehends the intelligible forms and values, implicit even in physical and bio-logical reality, as the inner principle of its order. Indeed, this intuition plays an important part even in that abstraction of conceptual data upon which the sciences are founded.[2] The soul is one, not mani-fold; and in normal human knowledge the three epistemological modes—sensible intuition or sensa-tion, discursive and analytic reasoning, spiritual intuition or intellect (aptly so-called, as in truth an 'inward-reading,' *intus legere*, of the significant

[2] See below, pp. 61-62.

forms implicit in the more superficial phenomenon)
—co-operate in varying proportions.[3] Nevertheless
the positive sciences are pre-eminently the work of
the analytic and discursive reason. As such they must
assume postulates, and can yield no information as to
ultimates, *e.g.*, the nature of matter, force, life, mind
or the origin and finality of the universe. The remark erroneously said to have been made by Laplace,
when asked by Napoleon why in his astronomy he
had made no mention of a Creator—'I had no need
of that hypothesis'—is, therefore, whatever exception
may be taken to its tone, excellent science. Astronomy must assume the existence of the sidereal universe. It may indeed trace its history from a state
of maximum organisation through successive phases
of nebulæ, star-clusters and stellar systems to its present condition. And it may even forecast its future
development to some hypothetical end of cosmic
death. But as to the origin of this cosmic evolution
or any purpose underlying it astronomy must be
silent.

Moreover we must be on our guard against a too
hasty acceptance of current scientific hypotheses because they happen to support what is, or is supposed

[3] Wust's *'Sinnlichkeit,'* *'Verstand,'* and *'Vernunft'*; see *Dialektik des Geistes,* Bk. I, chs. 7, 8 (pp. 249, *seq.*, 276, *seq.*).

to be, divinely revealed, or more generally to favour religion. For example, it is tempting to accept as the complete final truth Sir James Jeans's picture of an ageing universe. Does it not bear out the literal truth of that sublime Scripture which contrasts with the eternity of the Word the mortal stars: 'They all shall wax old as doth a garment . . . but Thou art the self-same and Thy years shall not fail'? Perhaps —and yet already Professor Millikan assures us that in the laboratory of interstellar space some process of cosmic chemistry is rejuvenating the universe, which therefore, as far as science can tell us, would seem to have no beginning or end—its life eternally renewed, as cycle follows cycle. Which of these two hypotheses is true only scientific research can decide. Religion and philosophy can await the decision with equanimity. And as for our text—if for the universe as a whole there is no senility—the stars grow old in turn, and the complementary statement, 'like a vesture shalt Thou change them and they shall be changed,' possesses a literal truth which it would not possess under the alternative hypothesis. When in the Middle Ages 'science' as represented by Aristotle appeared to teach the incorruptibility of the heavenly bodies—this indeed in flat contradiction of the Biblical text—Catholic theology did not dispute its verdict in the name of revelation.[4] Again, Professor Eddington's denial that spatial extension constitutes the essential nature of matter makes it easier to accept St. Thomas's view—essential to his statement of transubstantiation—that quantity is not substantial but simply the primary accident of substance. But it would be unwise indeed to regard this as a scientific proof of the Thomistic thesis. Nor yet may we hail with a too certain delight the current astronomical hypothesis of a finite universe. A future astronomy may disprove the calculations and arguments by which the universe is at present regarded as a limited, if unimaginably vast, area of time-space. And in any case astronomy can never prove a finite universe. Beyond the universe open to our ken, others may exist cut off from the reach of any human instrument. If we hold the universe to be finite, our only sure ground must be philosophical; the intrinsic self-contradiction of an unlimited creation, a being contingent and relative but nevertheless infinite.

And relativity itself? Here we must carefully distinguish between the relativity of all finite being inherent in its contingence, and at its maximum in the inorganic matter furthest removed from God's

[4] Dorlodot: *Darwinism and Catholic Thought*, p. 153.

Absolute Being—a metaphysical truth established independently of any hypothesis or confirmation by the physical sciences—and relativity as an astronomical hypothesis which may yet be replaced by what I may term with an oxymoron a relative absolutism, that is to say, by the hypothesis that time-space and its measurements are within the physical sphere of reference absolute, however relative with reference to that spiritual order of which the physical sciences can make no report. Further, we must, if we are to face the facts honestly, admit that the report of physical science is not always so immediately helpful to religion. Astronomy, for example, reveals a universe in which, so far as we can discover, life, and *a fortiori* mind, is confined to a few specks, in an all-but unbounded ocean of inorganic matter. Is this prodigious surplus of blind mechanism, this seemingly purposeless waste, what we should expect in the Creation of Divine Wisdom? No doubt the materialist must face the counter-difficulty, why and how, in this ocean of inorganic matter, vital and rational phenomena have made their appearance. But the fact remains that astronomy in its present state does appear to show an unaccountable dysteleology in the material universe. It may be that spirits can exist where life as we know it cannot. It may be that solar systems are more frequent than science will at present allow. It may be that the measured distances are but relative. Or it may be that God squanders this quasi-infinite waste of matter to show of how little worth are inorganic matter and mere quantity, as compared with life and mind with their qualitative values.[5] In any case, the mind that can measure a universe of matter is self-evidently of greater value than the unintelligent and lifeless vastness it measures.

From all this it is clear that if the physical sciences cannot disprove the data of philosophy and religion, they cannot prove them. To look to science to justify and permit religious belief—the attitude of mind that exclaims with a relieved joy: 'There really is a God, Professor Jeans tells me so; my will is free, Professor Heisenberg detects indeterminacy among the electrons; I actually can pray, Professor Oliver Lodge has given his sanction'—is not merely undignified and, as we have seen, perilous; it is radically unphilosophical. To base religion on science involves the same illicit extension of the province of the latter as the older rejection of religion as unscientific. Metaphysical reasoning on the other hand

[5] Inorganic matter does of course possess qualitative value also, for it possesses 'form.' But as compared with the qualitative values of life and mind it represents quantity rather than quality.

may anticipate a conclusion of physical science.
Relativity, as General Smuts has pointed out in his
presidential address to the British Association
(1931), has replaced 'the mechanistic world view'
of nineteenth-century science by 'the mathematician's
conception of the universe as a symbolic structure.'
But when science was still wholly wedded to mechanism, Newman on metaphysical considerations sug-
gested in a sermon preached in 1843 the economic
symbolism which has replaced it in the following
century. 'What if . . . the laws of physics are
themselves but generalisations of economical exhibi-
tions.' He even concluded almost in the very language of Professor Whitehead that the Copernican
and Ptolemaic astronomies were perhaps mere practical economies, neither true absolutely.[6]

Religion and metaphysics may indeed find in the
facts disclosed by science, and even in hypotheses
which however inadequate and incomplete are at
least partially true, reflections and analogies of their
distinctive truths. And they will always welcome in
the results of the sciences a revelation of God's
work on the lower plane of His creation. St. Augustine, absorbed in the contemplation of God and the

---

[6] *University Sermons*, xiv. *Theory of Development*, pp. 350-1
(ed. 1843).

soul, would know nothing besides. 'Whoso knoweth both Thee and them [the truths of astronomy] is not the happier for them, but for Thee only. Men go on to search out the hidden powers of nature which to know profits not. Who sees not how content we should be to be ignorant of the hidden mysteries of heaven and earth?' [7] This limitation, which defined the province of human thought and interest for centuries to come, was as a temporary restriction invaluable. If the modern preoccupation with the positive sciences and their practical fruits has so largely obscured man's spiritual vision, we can readily understand how disastrous the scientific progress of modern times would have proved before the doctrine of God and the soul, knowledge of the supreme spiritual realities, had been explored by the devotion and speculation of Christian saints and thinkers, and the results securely housed in the teaching and living witness of the Church. Only when that work had been accomplished could physical science develop without blinding men entirely to the world of spirit. Even the corresponding restrictions of the temporal and spatial framework of human vision to a universe some six thousand years old, and no more

[7] *Confessions*, v. 7. x, 35. *Solil.* i, 11-7. *Enchir.*, ch. 16. The attitude of Plotinus was the same. See *Enneads*, 3, 8, 6.

extensive than a compact system of sun, planets and stellar heaven revolving around a central earth was of great service to man's spiritual life and knowledge. On such an artificially limited stage the mind's eye, which otherwise might have lost itself in those infinities of time and space, whose prospect Pascal would later find so terrific, was concentrated on the supremely important drama of redemption, of man's union, individual and social, with God, in a word, his deification. Otherwise, Western thought might have succumbed to the formless pantheism of Indian speculation, whose pendent is the measureless æons, mahayugas, manvantaras, kalpas, of Hindu and Buddhist cosmology; or, defeated by the material immensities, might have measured the worth of man, not by the intrinsic nobility of his spirit and its capacity for God, but by his physical insignificance. But however salutary this restriction of interest, it could not be and ought not to have been permanent. Knowledge of God and itself once secure, the mind could look directly at the phenomena of physical and biological nature. St. Augustine's argument, if a happy error, was nevertheless fallacious. Could we know God as He is, we should indeed have no need to know creatures as well—not even our own soul. We should know them better in Him. But on earth, where we cannot see God, we add to our knowledge and to our knowledge of God, by knowing sensible phenomena, both in the experience of everyday life and more profoundly in the truths discovered and systematised by the sciences. Every new truth learned, be its object a physical element or some humble form of organic life, is indirectly an addition to our knowledge of the Divine Creator.

Moreover the sciences have an important function to perform in the service of religion; indeed, of metaphysics also. Among the many contributions to religious thought made by the late Baron von Hügel was his powerful perception of the spiritual and intellectual purification which the positive sciences might effect for the religious man. Though science cannot, as we have seen, tell us anything directly of God, it can by its disclosure of the reign of impersonal law, cleanse the justifiable and necessary anthropomorphism of religion from the false anthropomorphism which sees in God a magnified man arbitrarily interfering with every detail of the natural processes. Such an attitude, too common hitherto, is radically incompatible with the mentality produced by the study of the positive sciences. But who dare call its disappearance a loss for religion? God is greater, not pettier, than impersonal law.

By bringing home the magnitude of the part played by impersonal and unintelligent forces, physical and biological, the modern development of positive science has no doubt emphasised the extent and magnitude of the problem of evil. Where our ancestors were content with a more facile explanation of suffering and evil conduct as always the expression, penalty, or direct consequence of wilful sin, we realise to-day, as never before, how suffering and internecine strife prevailed throughout the vast epochs which preceded the advent of humanity, how heredity and environment, and the subconscious operation of instincts unrecognised by the agent himself, so enmesh the individual that his will is at every turn overweighted and overborne, how much suffering not merely does not, but in the circumstances cannot, produce a countervailing spiritual good. And men turn in despair to such irreligious pessimism as we find, for example, in the novels of a Thomas Hardy.

Here, too, there is no going back. Because the positivist enlightenment, in showing us the power of unintelligent forces, has too often, by the natural reaction which in our partial and jerky human progress accompanies every advance, become blind to the spiritual Personality behind and beyond, we may not reply by a blindness in the opposite direction. We must rather find an outlook sufficiently wide to embrace both these complementary aspects of reality. Such an outlook is provided by Catholic theology and philosophy when their implications are boldly worked out and defects of presentation due to the scientific immaturity of an earlier age removed. In his most profound study of the problem of evil, Father Joseph Rickaby, S.J., has argued that the defect of the lower levels of being—physical and even biological—intrinsically involves evil. Therefore, since even God cannot effect what is inherently impossible, He could not have created a universe embracing such orders of being without the presence of evil. Nor could He create human free will without sin arising sooner or later. 'The element of nothingness enters into every created being. This element means defectibility and consequent proneness to evil. God cannot create a creature free from this element of nothingness and defectibility, for He cannot create a creature that shall not be finite. . . . We may plausibly conjecture that it would be impossible for God, because against the nature of things, to create a universe . . . with no evil, physical or moral, anywhere. Such an all-blameless universe is an impossibility, as much as a round square

triangle is an impossibility. The element of Nothingness . . . must issue in evil somewhere. This is
the necessity of evil, rooted in the very nature of
finite and created things, and not to be eliminated
thence, even by the wisdom and omnipotence of
God.' [8] God, though in Himself infinite and absolute, cannot be so in finite and relative creatures.
And the more limited and relative they are, the less
can He be so in them. Hence physical and even biological laws, while revealing God's will to the extent
of their positive being, are so limited and deficient
that their order is and must be partial disorder when
judged even by the law of human reason. The Divine
Face is indeed mirrored in these depths of partial
being—but the lineaments grow fainter as we descend. And if the discoveries and methods of modern science were not needed to inform us of this,
they have been, and are—such is the limitation of
human nature—necessary to make us realise it. A
Catholic philosopher like Wust can exaggerate the
order of sub-human creation, as though the chaos of

---

[8] *In an Indian Abbey,* Conversation X, especially p. 120, also
Appendix A. It cannot of course, be *proved* that a world without
evil involves an intrinsic contradiction; if it could, the problem
of evil would be solved. But the alternative is the belief that an
all-wise and perfectly loving God could, if He so willed, have
produced all the positive values of the Universe, without the
concomitant evil, yet has not done so. This surely is a contradiction in terms.

matter-energy bordering on sheer nothingness were there wholly subdued to form, whereas it breaks through in an irrationality and evil,[9] an apparent lack of design, in strange contrast with the teleology which even the inorganic in certain aspects displays, and which on the biological plane achieves miracles of adaptation. And this element of disorder, which led Plato or his master Socrates from an earlier hope that all physical phenomena possess a complete teleological justification,[10] to the realisation that 'evils hover of necessity around mortal nature and this earthly sphere,'[11] the element of relatively formless energy yet unconquered by the advance of form, also appears in the grotesque ugliness—sometimes, so close is the intertwining of positive being and its negation, in fantastic conjunction with a bizarre beauty—not only of those primæval monsters long since extinct, but of many lower forms of life still surviving: loathly parasites, tape-worms, slugs, millipedes, octopuses, jellyfish. To many observers, indeed, these creatures seem beautiful, and that also with truth. No creature is wholly formless, and in so far as a creature expresses form it is beau-

---

[9] As *positive being* even this minimum of reality is good: irrational and the source of evil only in its deficiency.
[10] *Phædo*, 97-8.
[11] *Theætetus*, 176.

tiful. Nevertheless there is in material creatures an element of formlessness which, if practically negligible in the highest of these, a beautiful human body, is sufficient in many of the lower creatures—as indeed in human deformities—to outweigh for most observers the positive form and its beauty and thus produce in them an apprehension of repulsive ugliness. In such cases we are conscious of a deformity that appals by its revelation of the primordial chaos insurgent beneath the order superimposed. And if this peculiarly repellent ugliness is absent from inorganic nature, it is because it lacks life. Because it is inorganic,[12] its comparative lack of form does not contrast with the higher degree of formation which an organism implies. A rock or billow is beautiful in its simple contours. Could they come to life they would be hideous, creatures of nightmare. Perhaps the quickest way to realise this disconcerting blend of design and chaos, rationality and irrationality, cooperation and ruthless conflict, in the last resort of being and lack of being, is to study the behaviour of those insects—bees, wasps, ants and termites—in whom biological instinct, as the principle of a social organisation, has achieved its maximum.

[12] Even the 'inorganic' is, as Lossky shows, in its degree organic. But as compared with the biological organism it may be called inorganic.

Yet here also there is no justification for any radical pessimism, nor even for any disparagement of these lower physical and biological orders and the sciences which study them. Religion need not turn away from these inferior levels of being with disdain or fear. They are not evil as the Manichees held, nor mere illusion as Vedanta [18] teaches.

Everywhere as we climb the ladder of being, the positive, orderly and good increasingly prevails over the negative, chaotic and evil. Life organises the physical elements in its service and bends their mechanical laws to fulfil its inherent teleology. The harmonies become more complex and more subtle, the co-operation more elaborate, unity manifest in and through an increasing multiplicity. No doubt in consequence of inherent limitation, advance and gain in one direction involve regression and loss in another. For example, the cellular complexity essential to all but the simplest organisms involves natural death, unknown to the unicellular organisms that multiply by fission. But death will be followed by the advent of sex—a richer and more intense mode of union than the bonds of gravity or relative position, or the chemical combinations that preceded it. Nor is death a great evil for beings whose value is

[18] The *advaita Vedanta* of *Sankara*.

specific rather than individual. There is a balance of gain and progress, and when the advance of life has reached a blind alley in one direction—for instance, in the production of saurian monsters too bulky for their intelligence—it strikes out in another direction where the achievement will be greater. The scientist thus watches the Spirit moving over the waters to give form and life, that higher and more interior form. And if the work seems slow because these lower types of creature oppose the passive resistance of their deficient being to God's organising, moulding and lifegiving work, our measurements are of no account in the Divine eternity.

TECHNOLOGY; THE ETHICAL AND SOCIAL SCIENCES; HISTORY

IF by the violet band the positive sciences of matter and life are symbolised, and, as we shall see later, by the blue the intuitions of intellectual truth on which metaphysics and its subordinate branches of theoretical philosophy are founded, the intervening indigo will represent those practical sciences which order man's individual and social life. For these sciences are applications of ideal principles apprehended by intuition to the concrete phenomena studied by the positive sciences.

Among these practical sciences are those which shape material objects for human use—technology in all its branches. The enormous advance made by these in the machine age which opened in the eighteenth century has so dazzled its contemporaries that many have lost sight of anything beyond, have allowed the machine and the conveniences and comforts it produces to dominate their entire outlook.

Others, by a reaction easily intelligible, have tended to regard the machine and the industrial organisation based upon it as in itself evil, anti-spiritual or anti-vital, and indulge vain lamentations for the loss of an imaginary golden age in the past—truly a cry for the moon. Most valuable between these extremes are the considerations on the nature and justification of machinery which Mr. Christopher Dawson has given us in his essay, *Christianity and the New Age.* The machine and its achievements cannot be scrapped. Abolish the machine and the entire fabric of modern civilisation must crash in ruin with the removal of its foundation. The machine is, on the contrary, a signal triumph of mind over matter, and the progress of modern industry, which Mr. Dawson terms 'a scientific intellectualisation of nature,' 'corresponds in the natural order to the spiritual restoration of human nature which is the work of Christianity in the supernatural order.' In itself no doubt the machine order is spiritually lifeless because it is not inspired by and subservient to a higher spiritual order. But it may none the less be the 'body' which God has, largely by the unintentional labour of secularists and positivists, 'prepared' for the inhabitation of his lifegiving Spirit. And meanwhile there are those who, holding fast to religious belief and the sovereignty of spiritual values it involves, can still see in the machine and the organisation of labour and finance which it produces a reflection and effect of Creative Wisdom moulding to rational ends the chaos of physical energy. That man should control the forces of nature is indeed not enough, but it is a triumph of order, and as such in entire harmony with and of service to the establishment of a higher order, his co-ordination with his fellow-men and subordination to God and to whatever social hierarchy He has directly or indirectly sanctioned. Indeed it is only when man has achieved control over things that he is able to embody in his social order ideal and spiritual principles. Law, for example, can become juster and more merciful when the means of communication render the policing of society more efficient than when the criminal stands at least an equal chance of escape. And the economic lot of the majority can be improved without prejudice to the higher culture, hitherto necessarily confined to a small leisured class, only when machinery and an efficient system of distribution enable goods to be produced cheaply and in large quantities. The glaring contrast between the sublime political and social ideals of mediæval thought and the actual conditions of constant warfare and brutal savagery was due to the lack of sufficient organisation at the basis of mediæval culture. We shall therefore see in the machine and its effects not the transitory evils of their abuse, but a positive embodiment of spirit and possibilities for its service. On the other hand, the machine must always be the servant of man, not his master. When machines have been exploited to the utmost to perform their 'servile work,' there will remain the work which must bear the personal stamp of the craftsman. Wherever the machine would be not the tool but the substitute of individual design, its use must be rejected, even if economically more profitable—unless indeed the article be of such necessity that a supply is indispensable beyond the power of handicraft to provide at a cost possible to the consumer.

Ethics, the science which orders individual conduct, comprises two factors, the one contingent and variable, the other absolute. The absolute factor of ethics consists in the intuition of moral and spiritual values whose intrinsic worth is independent of the changing conditions of human life. Thus courage is as such a value, cowardice a negation of value; benevolence, gratitude and justice are values, malevolence, ingratitude and injustice negations of value.

It is the same with temperance, the control of the lower by the higher, and the sacrifice, when necessary, of the former to the latter, a law implied by the existence of a hierarchy of being. Max Scheler has propounded an ethic based on the immediate perception of values, an ethic of material, as contrasted with formal, value, a *materiale Wertethik*. He makes out a scale of values and their negations self-evident to ethical perception.[1] On the lowest rung of the ladder are the hedonic values and their opposites, the pleasant and the unpleasant, to which are subordinate the utility values which provide pleasure, and the luxury values which dispense it. Above these are the vital values and their opposites, the noble and the common or mean. To these are subordinate such values as health and youth. Above these again are the intellectual-spiritual values, embracing intellectual values in the stricter sense, truth and its acquisition, æsthetic and ethical values, including of course the perception of this value-scale and practical conformity with it. To these are subordinate and ministerial the values of positive science, technique and culture. Finally, at the summit of the ladder, is the distinctively religious value,

[1] *Der Formalismus in der Ethik und die materiale Wertethik*, II, 507 *et seq.*

holiness, and its contrast, profanity or secularity. Here of course is the sphere of distinctly religious ethics, as, for instance, the truth that virginity chosen for the love and service of God and as a means of special union with Him is a higher value than marriage and parenthood. If this *a priori* scale of values provides the framework of material ethics, its formal principle is the law of love, the obligation upon the will to choose higher in preference to lower values, the whole in preference to the part, therefore to love one's neighbour as oneself, and God above all besides.

The material ethic of values perceived and the formal ethic or duty of love constitute together and inseparably what I have termed absolute ethics. Such an ethic, however, is insufficient. The law of love cannot be accomplished in the same way under different conditions. Nor is the concrete embodiment of values identical in every time and place, for every individual or society. Hence the second factor of morals, contingent and relative ethics. The perception of values and the law of love, absolute ethics, belong to the zone of spiritual-intellectual intuition symbolized by blue. The changing conditions, fundamentally physical and biological, in which they must be embodied and realised, belong to that lower sphere discussed under the symbol of violet. It is for this reason that we have represented ethics by indigo.

If a concrete ethical system is regarded as absolute and the variable factor denied, a dead legalism will result when the conditions have materially changed. And in this change of conditions we must include changes of belief or knowledge in any sphere, religious, social, economic, scientific. Revolt against such a legalism is likely, from the partiality and one-sidedness of all human advance, to issue in a total or partial rejection of absolute ethics—ethics being regarded as altogether, or to a greater extent than is the case, the product of temporary and local conditions. Thus, for example, when Greek speculation perceived for the first time that the accepted code of morality was in part a customary and traditional code reflecting the habits, circumstances, prejudices and superstitions of a particular people and epoch, the Sophists rushed to the conclusion that morals are nothing but custom; as Herodotus put it, though he himself did not wholly reject absolute ethics, 'of all things established custom (νόμος) is king.' And a similar excess has not been wanting in modern times. It is, indeed, the ethical counterpart of the epistemological scepticism which, because human knowledge always contains a subjective factor, declares it wholly subjective or more subjective than it is. Absolute ethics corresponds to the positive being of creatures, particularly of humanity, relative to the deficiency and partiality of their being.

Metaphysically, though in practice the distinction is unimportant, we must distinguish within absolute ethics an element representative of eternal and absolutely immutable values and an element whose constancy and immutability arise from values inherent in human nature as such and under all circumstances, though not strictly absolute. That is to say, the term *absolute ethics* is employed in a wide sense, not always literally accurate. In fact, the only absolute ethics *in the strictest sense* is the law of love: the supreme duty of loving God, and the duty of loving creatures in proportion to their worth, irrespective of individual interest or liking—a duty expressed, so far as our fellow-men are concerned, by the command to 'love my neighbour as myself.'

In so far as concrete ethics are affected by the circumstances of a private individual within a given social complex, the individual application of the ethical rules relative to that particular society and period—which, though in that sense relative, are for the individual absolute—constitutes a further and more relative ethic, individually, as opposed to socially relative. To determine this individual ethic is the object of the indispensable but much decried science of casuistry. Casuistry, however, because it is a science, does not, strictly speaking, deal with the individual, but with a specific situation in which X, Y or Z may happen to be placed, and therefore cannot extend to the utmost degree of ethical relativity, where purely individual idiosyncrasies enter into the question. Here only the individual conscience with or without the advice of others can decide.

To the practical ordering of individual conduct by the application of absolute norms to relative and changing circumstances—absolute and relative ethics united in a concrete whole—corresponds an ordering of social conduct, also a combination of absolute norm and relative application. This is the science of politics in the widest sense, as the ancients understood it, including what is now called sociology and its subordinate science, economics. Since the sole object of economics is man's material well-being, the relative element is here at its maximum, the absolute at its minimum, little more perhaps than the principles of justice and function.[2] If no form of political

[2] See below, pp. 48-49.

organisation can possess absolute validity, still less
can any form of economic organisation. The Divine
right of capitalism or collectivism would be a doctrine even more absurd than the Divine right of
monarchy or democracy. If the societies of Christendom have been feudal or capitalist, in the theo-
cratic republic established by the Jesuits in Paraguay [3]
though sufficient private ownership was maintained
to safeguard the freedom of the individual and fam-
ily, the economic system was a Christian Socialism—
the means of production and distribution being for
the most part possessed and organised by the public
authority, central or local. The utmost that can be
maintained is that whatever social or economic
arrangement is based on the intrinsic nature of man
possesses as such that secondary or relative absolute-
ness which belongs to ethical rules similarly constituted. Since, for example, some social authority
invested with the power of coercion is necessary for
man as he is and will be to the end of human history, there is a Divine right of lawful authority,
whether vested in monarch, oligarchy or democracy.
But the scope of its authority to which that sanction

---

[3] See the description and appreciation of this Jesuit State, a
veritable earthly Paradise, in R. Fülop Miller's book, *The Power
and Secret of the Jesuits*, pp. 283-302, 'Under [the] guidance
[of the] Jesuits in Paraguay . . . the ideal Communist state came
into being' (p. 302).

extends will vary with the conditions of time and place, being such as is *necessary* to maintain social order under those particular conditions. Similarly, since men in all circumstances require for the due performance of their functions some private property, of which they can freely dispose even at the risk of abuse, there is a Divine right of private ownership, whose extent, however, is again determinable by the degree to which, in given circumstances, it is necessary for the free performance of function. The voluntary communism of religious orders is essentially conditioned by its religious reference, and therefore belongs, like virginity in individual ethics, to the supernatural order. In fact we might even lay down the axiom: dominion (ownership) founded on function. Function requires and justifies dominion. And function is of course organic. It is the activity, not of an isolated individual, but of the member of a social organism whose agent he is, though, being a rational person, he is within due limits a free and responsible agent. Function however does not demand and in ordinary conditions cannot even admit the principle of equal ownership, whether as between individual members of the same society, or members of different societies or at different times. Neither does justice demand any other

equality than that of opportunity, that is to say the
eligibility of any individual and his enablement, by
the necessary training and equipment, to perform
whatever function best suits his capacity. It was the
work of eighteenth and nineteenth-century Liberalism to emancipate the individual from a political
and social context which had been outgrown, and
which unduly confined his activities. It set him free,
though in practice very incompletely, to fulfil and
express his capacity. But, unfortunately, Liberalism
failed to provide the organic society within which
human activity becomes what it should be, a fulfilment of function. The activity and resources of
individuals were allowed to develop indefinitely
without reference to the good of society as a whole;
it was the unlimited growth of a cancer, not the
limited growth of a healthy cell. The old organism
was destroyed—and rightly, for it was too narrow
and too senile—but no new organism took its place.
Hence Liberalism produced an empty framework of
social freedom, which must be supplied with an
organic content if this framework in itself good is
not to be destroyed by new despotisms from the right
or left.

But we must not expect the impossible. The absolute ideals of function and justice can never be more

than partially realised. They can never be embodied perfectly in any political or economic arrangement, nor even relatively to the permanent characteristics of human nature. Concrete obstacles of physical environment, pre-existing arrangements, scientific ignorance, even ineradicable prejudices, traditions and customs, whose overthrow would involve greater evils than their maintenance, prevent anything but a gradual and always imperfect approximation to the ideal. Much has been written of the interaction of ideal and real factors, of force and righteousness. Never can one of these two factors completely determine a human society. For that, man must be morally perfect and absolute master of his physical environment. This is the reason why even Christianity has tolerated institutions falling far short of the social ideal—for example, slavery and judicial torture—and still tolerates war. As Don Luigi Sturzo has shown in his profound treatise *The International Community and the Right of War*,[4] war, though incompatible with the perfect fulfilment of the Christian law of love, has been permitted because in the actual state of international society it has been inevitable, and will become, as slavery is already, absolutely illicit only when society has de-

---

[4] Chs. 11, 12, 13. See especially pp. 203-7, 224-5.

veloped, as we hope it is in process of developing, machinery for the peaceful settlement of international disputes as efficient as its legal machinery for the settlement of disputes between individuals and subordinate corporations. Always the same inter-texture of absolute and relative, the indigo between the blue of absolute truth and right and the violet of actual conditions.

But a society may deliberately turn away from the highest values and organise itself on their rejection in favour of some lower and partial value: for example, Fascism on the basis of an absolute value ascribed to the national State, and Russian Communism, which not only, like Fascism, deifies the State, but makes this omnipotent society the active instrument for the propagation of a materialist atheism which proclaims that man is but an intelligent animal, and his sole good an efficient and equitable distribution of earthly possessions and enjoyments. A portent without historical precedent: the Soviet Union, a vast social organisation embracing in its sway one-sixth of the land surface of the globe, founded on the denial of spirit—yet maintaining itself more successfully than the revolutionary movements of the past. Nor can we be sure it will finally prove a failure. Efficient organisation and enthusi-

CANISIUS COLLEGE LIBRARY
BUFFALO, N. Y.

astic service may carry it through to success, at whatever cost of suffering and injustice to individuals. The spectacle weighs heavy on faith. Here surely is no reflection of God in human society, but a blatant challenge and denial. We must bow our heads to the inscrutable providence of God, as the Jews when Nebuchadnezzar sacked their city and temple and carried them captive to Babylon, and they could not, apart from faith in obscure prophecy, foresee that this destruction of their national state would be the means of purifying and firmly establishing Judaism as a Church, and thus preparing the way for the Messiah and the world Church He was to found. We may, however, remark that, whatever the official creed of Bolshevism, Marxism is not and cannot be what it professes to be, pure materialism. It is essentially an idea, an intellectual force. It represents in fact the wedlock effected by the Jew, Karl Marx, between two factors of wholly diverse provenance. One was a Hebrew longing for social justice, with the belief in its apocalyptic fulfilment—the desire and belief which fill the pages of the Prophets and proclaim their satisfaction in the jubilant notes of the Magnificat, *Esurientes implevit bonis et divites dimisit inanes.* The other was

the atheistic materialism of Feuerbach.[5] And it is
to the former, the positive and true inspiration, that
Bolshevism owes whatever value it may contain or
achieve. To the latter, the negative and false inspiration, it owes only its failure to satisfy or serve the
highest needs of the human spirits. Thus one aspect,
the positive and dynamic aspect, of Marxism is an
ethical *ideal*. That is to say, there is a metaphysical
contradiction at its heart whose logic must finally
work itself out. The Soviet may by a rigorous cen-
sorship starve the minds of its subjects. It cannot
prevent them thinking and therefore detecting this
fundamental inconsistency between a materialist philosophy and an intellectual and ethical ideal. Nor
can the religious capacity and need of the human
soul be silenced, though its voice be temporarily
stifled. In any event Bolshevist Communism cannot
prove more successful than the power which, repre-
senting as it did, the deification of triumphant force,
was for the seer of Patmos the Scarlet Woman, the
mother of abominations. Yet the sway of Imperial
Rome was due to the element of positive good in
its empire, and its victory a preparation for the
advent and triumph of the Christian Church. So

[5] See Baron von Hügel, *Eternal Life*, pp. 304, 305.

with Bolshevism. Whatever success it may achieve[6] will be due to the desire, however perverted in expression, for social justice, and to the power not of matter but of mind to harness the forces of nature. And its destiny will be to serve the spirit which it denies. Here also, as with the positivist science and technique of which we have spoken earlier, the enemies of God's Kingdom are working unwittingly for its construction, preparing the social body of God's human incarnation.

Moreover, as events have already proved, economic success is possible only by the abandonment of strict communism. Stalin's latest policy tends, by its principle of unequal pay for unequal work, to substitute functionalism for a rigidly equalitarian communism. Only as a functional, not as a purely communist, society (whatever the label may be) can the Soviet possibly carry through its industrial programme. Nor can State despotism, whether Fascist or Bolshevik, be finally tolerable. A possible development may well be a militantly secularist state, or union of states, organised on a functional basis; and in this Fascism and the Soviet might join hands. The

---

[6] I am not implying that Bolshevism must in fact succeed. But, in our ignorance of God's purpose in its regard, I envisage a very distinct possibility—apparently most adverse to the cause of religion.

machinery of Big Business Capitalism would be easily taken over by an economic order of this kind. In this Marx was a true prophet. There would be a relentless warfare against religion organised in the Catholic Church. Religion would finally conquer, and proceed as its long-wanted soul to utilise and inform the functional, not communist, organisation which had proved itself economically successful. Thus did Christianity with its bitter foe, the empire of the Cæsars; or rather thus it attempted to do, and would have done but for the barbarian invasions, with the resultant anarchy and savagery.

If I have dwelt at a seemingly disproportionate length on the Soviet State and its prospects, my purpose has been to show how even the most irreligious and materialist society must in its own despite represent and aid the manifestation of spirit in matter, and the organisation of matter by spirit—and thereby reflect and subserve, willy-nilly, the revelation of God in human history. To realise the presence and power of light we do well to look for it where it shines most faintly under the darkest and densest cloud.

The sociological sciences, which study the best practical order of social life, depend for their data largely on the theoretical science which studies the actual order of the past—namely history. Here, above all, ideal and absolute principles have struggled for embodiment under the concrete conditions imposed by the context of physical, biological and psychological factors. Of all men the historian must look at his subject through indigo-tinted glasses. He must be a philosopher with steady sight of ideal values, the blue—yet always take full account of the irrational forces operative both within and without human nature, the violet. Though cultures embody an ideal principle, are indeed what Mr. Dawson has termed 'religion-cultures,' their material basis is the occupations of men conditioned in turn by their physical environment.[7] As the individual never displays a purely spiritual activity, neither is any culture the pure product of a spiritual belief. The idea must take flesh not *in vacuo* but of the mother earth—the physical conditions under which a culture arises.

Without concrete embodiment ideals remain ineffective and sterile. But that embodiment, determined, as it so largely is, by irrational agents, must always lose much of the ideal purity. This, as we have already shown from our glance at sociology, is inevitable *a priori*. But only the study of history

[7] Christopher Dawson, *Progress and Religion*, c. iii.

can sufficiently bring it home to us. Even the embodiment of religious truth is no exception to the rule. Christianity is not and cannot be a purely spiritual religion. *'Verbum Dei carnem non de nihilo, non aliunde, sed materna traxit ex carne.'* 'The Word of God took flesh not of nothing, not from some extraneous source, but from the flesh of His Mother.[8] We must not therefore be astonished to find the boundaries of the Church largely determined by the conquests of the Roman legionaries, the formulation of her doctrine dependent on the diffusion of particular writings at a given epoch, her moral theology influenced by the legal, social and economic systems of a particular environment and period, her government assisted, though more often hampered, by a political situation itself necessarily due to such irrational factors as geographical situation and the fortune of war. This is but to say that she is a living historical organism, not an artificial construction without roots in the solid but very earthy and often muddy soil. For every historical phenomenon, event or society is blent of the idea and the more or less recalcitrant material in which it takes shape, so that of every such phenomenon,

[8] Bede, *Hom.* iv, 49, quoted in the eighth lesson for Our Lady's feasts.

indeed of history as a whole, may truly be said what is true in the strictest sense of religious history —most true of the history of the Jewish-Christian Church—that it is a 'night wherein things heavenly are united with things of earth, Divine with human': *nox in qua terrenis cælestia, humanis Divina junguntur.*[9]

[9] *Missale Romanum,* from the *Exultet.*

BLUE

METAPHYSICS

THE colour of sky and sunlit sea, '*dolce color d'oriental zapphiro*,' in which Christian art has clothed her who is the Seat of Wisdom, and which surely were the fitting liturgical vesture for her feasts,[1] aptly represents Wisdom.

This is the higher wisdom of the intuitive intellect which directly apprehends intellectual and spiritual truths: the first principles of intelligibility; values and their hierarchy; the absolute factor of ethics and social science; the data and laws of number and figure on which the mathematical sciences are built up by discursive reasoning; the forms of physical objects apprehended in abstraction from their matter; ideas; concrete mental phenomena; such qualities as beauty and moral goodness; the soul; and in diverse modes and on various levels

[1] In Spain and at Downside Abbey blue is by special privilege the colour worn on the Feast of the Immaculate Conception. Would that its use were universal! Blue is the missing Pleiad in the sequence of liturgical colours.

God Himself. Except when its object is the soul or God—and then normally on occasion of, and accompanied by, the operations of sense and discursive reason—this intuition is not found pure and unalloyed. Hence it has been possible to deny its very existence and confuse it with the emotion which often accompanies it, as it also accompanies sensation and even at times discursive reasoning. That intuition is not emotion is proved by the fact that its operation may be dry and unemotional. To the traveller, after a sleepless night in the train, the Alps display their beauty. No emotional response is forthcoming. Yet he perceives quite clearly the quality of beauty in the landscape. The intuition of beauty is present, but devoid of the feeling with which it is normally invested. I visit a picture-gallery, ill or tired. The result is the same—an unemotional intuition of beauty. And a dry form of mystical intuition is a normal experience of mystics.

'In observing relations,' Dr. Lossky points out,[2] 'we often experience feelings . . . at times clearly defined—for instance, a feeling of strain when observing striking differences. . . . Needless to say, these feelings are not relations; their only connection with relations is that they arise on the occasion of the

[2] *The World as an Organic Whole,* pp. 20, 21.

latter.' Mathematical intuitions are no more emotional than the reasoning based upon them. The perception of mathematical truth cannot be ascribed to emotion. Is it then solely abstraction and ratiocination from the data of sense? Sense never displays the geometrician's circle; and, being an ultimate, it cannot be the conclusion of a chain of reasoning. What then of abstraction? There is a dual operation here—the apprehension, beyond the imperfect circle of sense, of the idea or inner form of the circle as such, and the formulation of concepts expressing in conjunction that global apperception. The former is the work of the intuitive intellect, only the latter of discursive reasoning. The idea of *circle* is thus not, strictly speaking, abstracted from its concrete embodiment, because it is not perfectly there. In and through and beyond the imperfect circularity of the concrete object, which is indeed an abstraction from it, an abstract aspect, the intuitive intellect directly apprehends the ideal circle. Wust would therefore seem justified in finding in the mysterious active intellect (*intellectus agens*) of the Thomist at least one aspect of intuition.[3]

'What then,' it may be objected, 'is intuition? You cannot explain its nature.' Neither could sensation

[3] *Die Dialektik des Geistes,* p. 273.

be explained to a pure spirit. Fundamental modes of cognition are ultimates. Intuition has already been defined as direct mental apprehension. Some intuitions are distinct, analogous to sight; for example, the intuition of mathematical truths. But their object is always abstract. Others are obscure but concrete contacts, analogous to touch. Such are the intuitions of the soul and God. An intuition at once distinct and concrete is impossible in this life; which possibly may be all that many opponents of intuition intend by their denial. The justification for grouping under the common term intuition two types of apprehension so different as these is the existence of intuitions intermediate between both, less distinct and abstract than the former, more obscure and concrete than the latter. Such are intuitions of the forms of concrete and complex objects, or of metaphysical entities such as contingence or necessity.

'Intuition proves nothing. Only logical demonstration is valid.' True, intuition does not *demonstrate*. As I have already pointed out, no ultimate, from God to physical energy, is demonstrable. But intuition '*monstrates*,' shows its object directly to those who look into their own experience for what is pointed out, or indirectly to those who will trust the experience of reliable witness. In the former case the 'monstration' is sufficient proof, in the latter the foundation of a reasonable belief. Can the existence of God be proved? Demonstrated, no. 'Monstrated,' yes.[4] What of my own personality as an abiding unitary self? The answer is the same. Or the objective reality of the physical data revealed by the senses? Once more the same reply. Upright and intelligent men have denied and do deny all these truths, and defy logical confutation. They are like a man who, unable to perceive the beauty of a picture or the moral worth of an act of virtue when it is pointed out, should demand a demonstration of its æsthetic or ethical quality. Only the most distinct and most abstract intuitions, *e.g.* intuitions of ultimate mathematical truths, compel assent from all men and under all circumstances because they alone are perfectly distinct. But even these are 'monstrated', not demonstrated.

Consider, for example, the five Thomistic proofs of Theism.[5] The first three of the five proofs set

[4] The metaphysical intuition to which this 'monstration' is addressed is, of course no act of faith in a supernatural revelation but an exercise of the human intellect by which man attains that 'certain knowledge' of God within the scope, as the Vatican Council defined, of his natural capacity. Nor does it imply the identification made by ontologism between the intuition of minimal being, common to all that exists, and the intuition of the Absolute Divine Being.

[5] *Summa Theol.*, I-II., *a.*, 3.

out in the *Summa*—from motion, efficient cause, and the possible and necessary—are ultimately reducible to one,[6] the argument from contingent or relative to absolute, necessary and self-existent being. Such an argument, however, is a monstration of absolute Being as implied in the contingency of created being as its source, ground and presupposition. It appeals to an intuition of contingency as implying an absolute, or, if you will, of the absolute as implicit in the fact of contingency. St. Thomas's fourth argument from the graduated perfections of being—that hierarchy of being and value of which we have spoken so much—to a perfect being and value presupposes the intuition of these values and their order. And his final argument—the teleological proof from design—is founded on an intuition of the principle of sufficient reason and the intelligibility of Order, with its implication—the priority of mind to matter. Kant's rejection of these proofs was due to his refusal to admit the objective validity of the metaphysical intuitions involved, particularly the intuition of the principle of causality or sufficient reason—a refusal that is, however, equally fatal to the objective reference of the positive sciences, and involves universal scepticism. These

[6] Rev. M. C. D'Arcy, S.J., *St. Thomas Aquinas*, pp. 160ff.

monstrations or showings are examples of what I
have termed the contemplative method. Wust, who
rightly sees in it the fundamental method of metaphysics, calls it the speculative method.[7] The mind
contemplates its object, and in that contemplation
discovers, though of course but partially, what it
essentially is and what are its properties and implications. The more fixed the contemplation, the more
deeply does the mind penetrate to the ultimate metaphysical facts and laws within and beyond the superficial phenomenon.

This is the reason why controversy, however
skilled and cogent, is so often barren. The opponent
will not or cannot see what you would show him.
Between himself and the object he places some other
object or some irrelevant aspect of the object in
question. Or he prefers the dictum of some authority—society, book, teacher or current belief—to the
use of his own intellectual eyesight. Or again, if
his own vision is in that particular defective, he is
too proud to admit the fact and to accept the vision
of others. Indeed, the object may be so obscure that
only the sight of a few spiritual or intellectual giants
can attain it. Or it may be invisible or not easily
visible from the point of view adopted by a particu-

[7] *Die Dialektik des Geistes,* p. 73.

lar intellectual milieu, epoch or culture. In this case faith in the testimony of others may be pre-requisite, for that shifting of the angle of vision which will bring the object within personal ken. Or a man—indeed a group—may refuse the necessary time and leisure to focus the vision. The short sight of bustling superficiality or rationalist cleverness will not easily adjust itself to the longer focus of metaphysical or religious contemplation. When M. Maritain tells us that the radical evil of the present time is the lack of contemplation he is, I venture to think, stating in its subjective aspect what I state from the objective when I urge as the most pressing need of the day the reaffirmation of the metaphysical order of being. For it is by contemplation, and contemplation alone, that the order of being is apprehended.

A procedure much in favour to-day attempts to explain a fact of experience such as the sense or rather intuition of beauty, belief in God, conscience, life or intelligence, as the sum or resultant of the conditions under which it appears or is believed to have arisen, or of the factors whose combination gave it birth. This is to argue that because I can see a particular view only by climbing a certain hill that view is the result of my ascent, or that water is nothing more than the summed properties of its component gases. Our safeguard against such perverities is the acceptance, as a channel of objective truth, of that highest activity of the human mind, intellectual intuition, combined with a reasonable trust in the well-attested intuitions of others. And, we need hardly say, the data of such intuition must not be divorced from the data of sensation and their testimony, and both must be exploited and controlled by logical inference.

The Englishman is notoriously unmetaphysical. For him, metaphysics is a veritable 'treading on emptiness high up in air.' [8] Man is, however, essentially a metaphysician—I had said a metaphysical animal, but that it is in being a metaphysican that he proves himself no mere animal. Long before they acquire sufficient experience to conceive a scientific order—when a lion may still appear from nowhere at the foot of the bed, and the parent is invested with a quasi-omnipotence, able at least to obtain all the money he needs by the simple process of calling for it at a bank—children will ask questions concerning the ultimate metaphysical realities. And a period of child-like naïvety in the sphere of physical or historical science—for example, the Middle Ages—

[8] Father Joseph Rickaby's brilliant emendation, completing Bishop Lightfoot's, of *Colossians,* ii., 18. See *Further Notes on St. Paul,* pp. 163 *sqq.*

may produce metaphysicians of unsurpassed scope and profundity. Every human experience involves metaphysical reality and its intuition. And the questions of most vital importance require a metaphysical answer. If metaphysical intuition be invalid all knowledge falls with it. And if metaphysics seems to play such a small part in human life, to be the exclusive province, or shall we say playground, of an unpractical minority, 'remote and ineffectual' like Mr. Belloc's Don, it is because popular metaphysics is implicit and unformulated, its intuitions never disentangled from their vehicles, sensation, tradition, custom, rules of practice, and religious doctrines. What we call common sense is largely implicit metaphysics. Conscious metaphysics, abstracted from this concrete context and systematised, arises partly from the need felt by a few minds to co-ordinate and classify their knowledge, partly out of attempts to explain experience by some partial aspect or category, and the reaction against it.

In fact the relation between scientific and popular metaphysics is the same as that between scientific theology and popular religion. And scientific theology is due to the same factors, systematisation and controversy, which produce scientific metaphysics. Indeed, scientific theology is very largely the formulated metaphysics of religion. Moreover, once conscious speculation has arisen, popular metaphysics is as inadequate as popular religion. To trust in either is to meet unarmed the armed forces of some partial philosophy or creed which has not disdained a scientific equipment. Hence the victories of Protestantism in the sixteenth century, when only a small minority of Catholics, even amongst the clergy, possessed an adequate knowledge of theology; or, in our days, of secularist positivism, with its plausible appeals to science.

The object of metaphysics, scientific or popular, far from being 'airy nothings' is, in a word, *ultimates:* ontological categories which cannot be analysed or explained in terms of anything else. They are often synthetic principles, for example, organic life. Only God and 'matter-energy' are ultimates in the sense that there is nothing beyond them. That is to say, metaphysics is concerned with the foundations of every branch of human knowledge and activity.

Even to deny metaphysics one must be a metaphysician. Positivism and Marxian materialism are based on a metaphysic—though woefully incomplete and inadequate. I use my physical senses, I am an animal. I use my intellectual sight, I am a metaphysician. And normally I am something of both in the same concrete perception. As for technicalities, the scientific account of sensation is at least as technical.

Another cause of the disparagement of metaphysics is a prejudice, by no means confined to Englishmen, but everywhere current since the rise of modern Positivist Rationalism, which impregnates the entire intellectual atmosphere of the modern West and colours the imagination and practical attitude of many who would theoretically reject its fundamental principle. This prejudice—the reverse of the Augustinian prejudice against sense-knowledge and positive science—is based on the assumption, expressed or tacit, that mind is less real than matter. Mental phenomena are regarded either as wholly subjective and illusory, or at most as secondary, pale reflections of solid material reality. The ideal is but the shadow of the material. And many Christians who are ready enough to admit that God is the most real Being, *Ens Realissimum*, fail to perceive the implication of this, and persist in regarding the mental or spiritual as less real than the physical. The exact contrary is the truth. Matter is but the shadow of mind, physical phenomena of spiritual noumena. And if such terminology of spiritual doctrine as *speech*, *silence*, *word*, *touch*, *sight*, *light*, *illumination*, *conception*, *birth* and *marriage*—indeed *spirit* itself, which is etymologically *breath*—is, and must necessarily be, in its origin, metaphor drawn from physical phenomena, in reality physical breath, speech, silence, word, touch, sight, light, illumination, conception, birth, and marriage are metaphors of their spiritual counterparts on a higher plane, images and shadows of the former which they reflect in a lower order of being. And created spirit is in turn a shadow of the Divine. To have imposed this truth on the thought of Christendom was the supreme merit of Augustine. Until this prejudice in favour of matter against mind, of the lesser against the greater realities, of the shadow against the substance, has been overcome, Western culture will never regain the intrinsic stability which alone can save it from internal disintegration, nor will modern man find the peace for which he is groping, the peace of order. And it can be overcome only by a thorough-going acceptance of the hierarchy involved in all religious faith, indeed, in the very existence of mind, in other words by that reaffirmation of the metaphysical order of being which is, it cannot be emphasised too strongly, our supreme and most urgent need.

'For lack of vision the people perish.' No society or culture can dispense with the vision of metaphysical truth. In simple societies and cultures the implicit metaphysics of common sense completed by the implicit metaphysics of religious belief may suffice. Only scepticism has awoken, still more when the positive method and temper of rationalist science has developed, a conscious and formulated, that is, a scientific, metaphysics becomes socially indispensable. The modern rejection of metaphysics in which Comte saw a proof of intellectual progress has produced an intellectual anarchy which leaves society and its civilisation without a principle of unification and co-ordination, and in its absence they must disintegrate, as surely as the body when its life-principle has departed from it. A bond of material interest and compulsion indeed remains. But how effective is it? How long will it endure? And the danger is urgent that such an aimless unprincipled society and civilisation will succumb to some partial metaphysic embodied and imposed by a powerful state or party, for example, Marxism, or the less coherent, if wider, ideology of Fascism. Nor can religion supply the place of metaphysics. For European society lost the government and inspiration of a common religion, even before it lost a common philosophy, objective and sufficient.[9]

If metaphysics be the science which studies the data of the intuitive intellect, its scope will be more extensive than what is usually called metaphysics, and will partially coincide with psychology, epistemology, logic, ethics and sociology. In all these disciplines it will provide the fundamental and absolute principles.[10] And if physics and biology are usually excluded from the sphere of metaphysics, it is only by confining them to the study of the subordinate manifestations of their respective principles, material energy and life. If the intuition of these first principles by their contemplative method were included in their scope, physics and biology would to that extent be annexed to metaphysics.

Æsthetics in all its branches represents a special department of metaphysics, for it is based on the intuition of æsthetic values, and secondarily on the ideas which a work of art or literature embodies. Any criticism, literary or artistic, which is not thus metaphysical is nothing more than an analysis of

[9] I do not mean one system accepted universally in every detail —but a common acceptance of the fundamental principles of every solid and comprehensive metaphysic.

[10] See above, pp. 44-45.

superficial technique, for example, a study of metrical pattern or the linear analysis of a picture. And even this culminates in the immediate 'monstration' of an æsthetic quality irreducible to anything beyond itself and apprehended by intuition. Moreover æsthetics involves psychology, and psychology in turn involves metaphysics, or more truly is in its profounder reach metaphysical psychology. For a psychology which is more than the mere registration of behaviour, nervous reaction to stimuli, the laws of association and other more or less superficial psychophysical sequences, is necessarily a metaphysical psychology—the metaphysics of the human mind. Indeed, such a metaphysical psychology, which of course includes that study of the nature and validity of human knowledge known as epistemology, has been the starting-point and centre of many systems of metaphysics, for example, the philosophies of St. Augustine and St. Bonaventure, of Descartes and Kant, however inadequate the procedure of the latter, and it was one of the foci of Platonism, if not also Aristotelianism. Metaphysical intuition thus plumbs the soul, that microcosm of all known creation, and takes soundings of its depths.

Nor is the human spirit the term of its endeavour, 'that with no middle flight intends to soar.' For if metaphysical intuition scans the foundations of human experience, it contemplates its supreme height and crown—God. For, in the first place, the ideas which it contemplates are ideas of the Divine Mind existing in the Word, the Form, that is, the living Exemplar, of all forms. The mind does not indeed contemplate the ideas directly in the Word. Such a direct contemplation would involve the beatific vision of God as He is in Himself. Plato appears to have entertained the hope that in this life he might attain a vision of the Good, that would enable him to explain phenomena by their ideas, thus directly understood; in other words, to achieve a deductive teleological science proceeding from above downwards and seeing the effect in the cause. In the *Phædo* Socrates expresses his disappointment when, instead of the deductive teleology he had expected, he found in Anaxagoras only an empirical science, content to establish laws of phenomenal sequence without attempting their teleological justification. 'I heard someone reading from a book of Anaxagoras that mind was the disposer and cause of all, and . . . I said to myself: if mind is the disposer, mind will dispose all for the best and put each particular in the best place; and I argued that if anyone desired to find out the cause of the generation or destruction

or existence of anything, he must find out what state
of being or doing or suffering was best for that thing.
. . . I rejoiced to think that I had found in Anaxagoras a teacher of the causes of existence . . . and
I imagined that he would tell me first whether the
earth is flat or round; and, whichever was true, he
would proceed to explain the cause and the necessity
of this being so and show that this was best. . . .
How grievously was I disappointed! I found my
philosopher altogether forsaking mind or any other
principle of order but having recourse to air and
ether, water and other eccentricities!' [11] Plato, however, seems still to have hoped for a vision of the
Idea of the Good which would yield the teleological
science of first causes with which he had not been
furnished by Anaxagoras. And the frustrated hope
of direct causal vision lingered on, at least as the
ideal of human knowledge, in spite of the Aristotelian reaction to direct physics, and no doubt was in
part responsible for the comparative lack of interest
in the positive sciences characteristic of antiquity,
and still more of the earlier Middle Ages—before
Platonic Augustinianism had yielded to the Aristotelianism of the Thomists. St. Augustine, it is true,
did not believe that our ideas are seen directly in the

[11] *Phædo,* 97-98 (Jowett).

light of God—'*in lumine Dei.*' It is only their truth
that is seen thus.[12] But his Neo-Platonism combined
with the religious preoccupation of his personal
interest to make him regard the knowledge of creatures in themselves as of little worth. With Thom-
ism came a reaction which denied intuition as a
human mode of knowledge or rather confined it
unduly to the first principles of intelligibility.

But if metaphysical intuition does not behold the
ideas as they are in the Word—living concrete reality, according to the profound and quite possibly
authentic reading of St. John's Prologue: 'Whatever
was made in Him was life,' it apprehends them in
objects as images or expressions of the primal Exemplar, therefore in the reflected light of the Word,
though not immediately in that light itself. Thus
contemplating the ideas, metaphysical intuition indirectly contemplates God. No doubt this is in a sense
true even of sensation, but the reflection of the
Divine Light is there at double remove, the reflection
of a reflection. And, as intuition penetrates the
hierarchy of ideas, it finally contemplates God Himself, the Idea of ideas, their Unity and Ground.
True, even this contemplation is a contemplation of

[12] E. Gilson, *Introduction à l'Étude de Saint Augustin,* Ch. v.,
especially p. 118 *seq.*

God in those primary ideas which are the various aspects under which creatures are related to Him, and He is thus apprehended in and beyond them, for example, as the Absolute presupposition of their contingencies, the sufficient reason of their intelligibility, the beauty reflected by their harmonies, the perfect good their partial values imply. And above this, again, intuition contemplates negatively God's utter transcendence of creatures, His absolute distinction from them, His entire otherness. Concrete intuition of God, and contact with Him as the living and active Godhead, belong, it is true, only to the mystical experience which wholly transcends the sphere of metaphysics. But that direct contact can be expressed only through metaphysical categories. If the subject of even sensible experience becomes in some degree a metaphysician as soon as he expresses his sensations, the mystic must be pre-eminently a metaphysician when he attempts to utter his spiritual experiences. And metaphysical preoccupation with the intellectual framework of Divinity invites its filling with its concrete content, direct union with God. It is not surprising that many of the world's greatest metaphysicians, Sankara, Ramanuja, Socrates (probably), Plato and Plotinus, Augustine, Bonaventure, and Thomas, have also been in varying measure mystics.[18] The blue of metaphysical intuition is indeed the blue of the heavenly vault.

[18] It will be seen that I admit the supernatural character of the mystical experience of the non-Christian philosophers. Its possibility is cogently argued by Père Maréchal, S.J. (*Studies in the Psychology of the Mystics,* pp. 276-277), though he would not apply the principle so widely as the present author.

For Plotinus, see Fr. Sharpe's *Mysticism, its Nature and Value,* pp. 156-157.

GREEN

LIFE

FROM the sky to homely earth, from depth of space mirrored in the expanse of ocean to the fields or gardens at our door, we descend in turning from blue to green. And in our symbolism we exchange the lofty apprehension of metaphysical intuition as it penetrates the profundities of the soul and gazes upward to God for the life of nature, vegetable and animal, including the vegetative and animal life in ourselves. We have returned from the metabiological to the biological. But whereas we have hitherto been mainly concerned with the contemplation which involves a certain separation from its object, we have now in mind a closer contact with the object, an immediate experience of its concrete actuality, a participation of its life, in short the complementary factor of concrete vital union. Indeed, the life, here so directly and concretely experienced, is in part our own, an aspect of our own nature and activity.

This biological life, in its various effects and embodiments, is the object of the nature-religions; those polytheisms which deify the elementary powers of nature. Even the inorganic is for the nature-religions regarded as alive: wind and sun and sea are as living as the plant or animal. No doubt a metabiological activity akin to that of the human spirit, a quasi-human personality, is ascribed to these nature deities. But so long as a nature-religion is unaffected by later speculations this rational humanity is subordinate and instrumental to biological life, its needs, pleasures and passions.

But although the object of the nature-religions is some manifestation or embodiment of natural life, yet inasmuch as they are religions even the nature polytheisms involve, in the religious acts they evoke, a reference, confused, obscure or unrecognised, to the supernatural Deity in but beyond nature, immanent in but transcending the biological order—involve, that is to say, a worship of the true, if Unknown God. Idolatry is distinguished from Image-worship by an undue finality. It rests in the relative as though it were the Absolute, worships the creature, the image and vehicle of the Divine Spirit, as though it were that Spirit. Hence the passage from Idolatry to Image-worship is not difficult for any sincerely religious pagan. Moreover even in primitive religions the sky-god, no doubt because of the physical elevation of his dwelling and its remoteness from earth, is invested with a spiritual, ethical, and absolute character, being regarded as the supreme and universal Father and Creator. Thus the most rudimentary forms of religion contain the germ and indistinct lineaments of a supernatural monotheism. The germ, however, very largely failed to grow; the outline became no clearer. On the contrary, the polytheistic nature-cults, as they developed, tended to thrust this primitive monotheism more or less completely out of sight.

In the East, Vedanta and even Buddhism, though the antithesis of nature-worship, have continued to incorporate it as a lower and preliminary stage of religion. With a sacred philosophy which rejects the life of nature even too exclusively the Hindu and Buddhist is able to combine a worship of its deified powers. Judaism, Christianity, and Mohammedanism have on the contrary faced nature polytheism with uncompromising hostility. Only thus could the supreme claim and truth of religion as essentially spiritual and metabiological be asserted with complete success. This necessary reaction against the worship of natural life, against the confusion which invested the biological with the value of spirit and even of Absolute Spirit, did not and could not escape the universal law of human reaction. It tended to depreciate unduly the positive and even religious value, that is to say, the holiness, of the manifestations, channels and embodiments of natural life as reflections of the supernatural and images of God. The public baths were abandoned to decay. Christian art was long marked by lack of interest in the beauty of the human form. The substitution of Byzantine mosaic for Greek sculpture was profoundly symptomatic of this change of outlook. Drama was long widely condemned, for example, by Bossuet in the seventeenth century. Such excesses, however, were but the inevitable reverse of the positive affirmation of spirit and its sovereignty, which was inspiration and the indispensable achievement of that religious movement of the later Empire which under Divine Providence made the Christian Conquest possible. The doctrines of the Incarnation, Eucharist and Resurrection have consistently maintained at the centre of Christian belief the holiness and worth of the body and its physiological life. An incarnational and sacramental religion cannot deny physical life and beauty. The Liturgy is never weary of praying for physical health, even in the penitential rite of Ash Wednesday. The Post-Communion for the sixteenth Sunday after Pentecost condenses into a few words a programme of psychotherapy.[1] And the subordinate worth and claims of physiological life as the necessary basis of the spiritual life in man have found full recognition from the most responsible Catholic thinkers of to-day. For there are not two vital principles in man—two souls—but one vital principle and one energy, which may be informed and directed either by a natural and biological or by a supernatural and spiritual purpose. The biological life with its distinctive quality and temperament, specific and individual, is the material—the immediate matter—which the spiritual will, itself moulded by the love of God, must inform and fashion. And the good artist respects his material.

But the natural life with which we are now concerned is, as I have said above, not only in man. It is the life of nature as a whole—the life that works in the leaves, blossoms in the flowers, moves and feels in the animals. Nor would I exclude those inorganic elements and forces on which life depends

---

[1] 'PURIFICA, *quæsumus, Domine,* MENTES NOSTRAS *benignus, et* RENOVA *cælestivus sacramentis: ut* CONSEQUENTER *et* CORPORUM *præsens pariter, et futurum capiamus* AUXILIUM.' '*Purify our minds,* we beseech thee, O Lord, in Thy loving kindness, and *renew* them by Thy heavenly sacraments, that *as a result* we may obtain both present and future *bodily help.*'

and which even seem themselves alive: the light of the sun, *il padre d'ogni mortal vita;* the wind, as it rides through the grass or sings among the foliage; water, as it advances in the exultant vigour of the sea waves, or rushes in foaming haste down the bed of the mountain torrent. The energy which fore-shadows life, life vegetative and subsentient, life mobile, fully sentient and sub-intelligent—these three form an ascent of natural force, inorganic and vital, developing and unfolding new marvels of power and beauty. And the unfolding of life is a sequence of increasingly complex organisms more subtly adapted to their environment and functions. And throughout, the energy-matter is moulded ever more perfectly by the form imposed upon it, a wed-lock of form and matter renewed in the generation and growth of every individual organism, and sym-bolised for the nature-religions by the marriage of the Mother Goddess, the energy substrate, with the Sky Father, the form that quickens that lower energy to organic life.

In thus speaking of an energy-matter formed to organic life, I am of course speaking comparatively. A totally unformed energy-matter cannot actually exist, it is mere potentiality. But the formed matter of one level becomes the matter of a higher form.

Inorganic energy-matter is the matter of vital form, life in turn of spirit.

Of the scientific study of the biological process and ascent we have already spoken. Here I have rather in mind its direct apprehension and enjoyment by sensible experience—not the botanical dissection of the dead flower, though that also is valuable, but the sight and it may be the smell of the living blossom. For the life thus experienced is a revelation of the living Author of Life—*deus vivus et vivificans.*

If the Word is the Ground and Exemplar of Form, the Spirit is the Ground and Source, the Mover and Giver of Life. His love is the supreme life, and His the creative brooding over chaos, till created life, that shadow of Himself, arises and unfolds. If the Liturgy is preoccupied with the work of the Holy Spirit as the source of supernatural life, it does not forget His function as the author of natural life. He is the *Creator Spiritus,* and it was natural life which the Psalmist had in mind when he wrote: 'Send forth Thy Spirit and they shall be created and Thou shalt renew the face of the earth.' A rugged but powerful sequence written by St. Hildegarde [2]—a mystic of

[2] In Prof. Phillimore's Anthology, *The Hundred Best Latin Hymns,* No. 40, pp. 58, 59.

marked cosmological interests—emphasises this aspect of the Spirit's work:

> *O ignis Spiritus Paracliti*
> *Vita vitae omnis creaturae*
> *Sanctus es vivificando formas.*

'Fire of the Paraclete, life, source of all life created, Holy art Thou giving life to the forms'—that is, creating the energy substrate, in which the Divine Ideas receive concrete embodiment and existence as created forms.

> *De te nubes fluunt,*
> *Æther volat,*
> *Lapides humorem habent,*
> *Aquae rivulos educunt,*
> *Et terra viriditatem sudat.*

From thee the clouds move, the air flies on its way, the stony rock exudes moisture and gives forth streams, and the earth puts forth the green herb.'

> *O iter fortissimum*
> *Quod penetravit omnia*
> *In altissimis*
> *Et in terrenis*
> *Et in omnibus abyssis,*
> *Tu omnes componis et colligis.*

'Most mighty traveller, thou dost penetrate all things in the heights above, on earth and every abyss'— those utmost depths and foundations, the matter whose action is laid bare by modern physics, and those obscure depths of life where another chaos of warring instincts is being moulded to an organic purpose. 'Thou dost gather together and arrange all.' Life is essentially organisation, order; and the higher the life, and the fuller therefore the communication of the life-giving Spirit, the more complex the organisation, the more perfect the order. The advance of energy, life, intelligence, is everywhere correlative with an advance of form, external arrangement of homogeneous parts, organic harmony of differentiated parts, rational order of developed instincts and functions; a correspondence indicated by Herbert Spencer's formula of evolution as the passage 'from an indefinite incoherent homogeneity to a definite coherent heterogeneity.' The Word and the Spirit are one God.

No doubt as the physical forces tend to oppose the higher purpose of life, and break away from its control in the disintegration of death, so as a result of the inherent limitation of creatures the exuberance of biological life tends to resist its moulding by a rational teleology ever stricter and more perfect. In nature we witness an internecine struggle of living organisms, and in man, so far as he lives by the biological laws of the flesh, an internal anarchy of uncontrolled and unharmonised passions, or the irrational tyranny of the most powerful amongst them, to which there corresponds an outer anarchy of suicidal strife between individuals, classes and nations, or the uncontrolled tyranny of one individual, class or nation. But the victory of spirit, if therefore slow and incomplete, is sure. Examples of marvellous co-operation and inter-adaptation mark in various directions the evolution of vegetable and animal life, a co-ordination and co-operation of parts in the individual or of individuals in the species—even, as in the phenomenon of symbiosis, between different species. And human history, for all the abuse it records of the free choice by which man must voluntarily execute the Will of love and life, displays signal victories of reason and self-sacrifice over irrational and egoistic instinct, whether individual or social.

Moreover, in this advance of being, law becomes increasingly intrinsic, identical with the inner law of the subject's nature. The physical particle is externally restricted by the interference of other particles. The plant obeys an intrinsic law of growth, the animal an instinct which determines its activity for the good of the species, even at times at the cost of its individuaal life. And if even the most interior of these laws is unfree, it is at least spontaneous, obeyed with no sense of constraint.

In man, because he belongs in part to the biological, in part to the metabiological, zone of being, there is no inner law which spontaneously determines and co-ordinates his behaviour. But his will, obeying freely the Spirit's law of love, may attain even on earth such supremacy that he follows that law without constraint as his highest good and the satisfaction of his desire. Here, far more than in the animal, law tends to become identified with spontaneity because spontaneity is now rational freedom. But everywhere external law enforced by compulsion is but the necessity of imperfection. As such it tends, as life develops and advances and ascends the scale of being, to yield to the inner and perfect law of liberty, *lex perfecta libertatis,* in which law and love are one.

Thus the struggle for existence is the law of life only in its positive aspect, the tendency of every living thing to maintain and assert its being. The inevitable reverse, competition against others, is but the imperfection of a life so remote from the full life of God, and the higher the form of life the more that negative aspect is subordinated to the positive law of love. Even in animal nature the sacrifices of motherhood and of those insect workers—bees or ants—who wear out their lives prematurely for their community, foreshadow the spiritual life that asserts itself triumphantly in loving surrender of the biological. 'He that loses his life shall find it.'

There have been, indeed still are, those who see in the theory of evolution as taught by Darwinian and post-Darwinian science a menace to religion. No doubt when interpreted in terms of a positivist and mechanical philosophy, evolution must appear to exclude God. But the illusion is dissipated when it is seen as a manifestation of Creative Spirit, the record of the Spirit's motion over the face of the deep. The mechanical operation of natural selection cannot account for the appearance of the variations it selects. And whatever the extent of the part it plays in evolution—on this point scientists differ widely—it determines at most which of these new essays of life shall survive. The struggle for existence is the expression of that factor of blind necessity with which the form, the creative manifestation of the Divine Idea, must contend in this lower world. And evolution is precisely the gradual overcoming of necessity, the progressive rationalisation and spiritualisation of matter which man's work continues on a higher plane.

Since the hierarchy of being is, as we have seen, a scale of degrees between nothingness and Absolute Being, we shall expect a continuity in their appearance. Up to the present there is no scientific proof of abiogenesis—the derivation of living from non-living matter. But St. Thomas accepted it as taught by the Aristotelian science of his day, and it is not easy to believe that the first living organisms were introduced into the world from without. Everything indicates that when the chemical organisation of matter attained a certain complexity, the organising form assumed that quality we call life, though it was a distinctive and novel quality, and as such a novel and fuller communication of the Spirit, made whenever and wherever a subject was prepared to receive it. The ascending complexities of chemical or biological factors may thus be compared to a series of increasingly powerful field-glasses or telescopes. The more powerful lens presents objects invisible to the less powerful, focusses them within the field of vision. But it does not produce them. Similarly, each superior complex of predisposing factors more elaborately combined focusses a brighter reflection of the Divine Light, a novel form which mirrors the Exemplar Idea in the Divine Mind, for example, a new chemical property or form of organic life. But this new light, this novel form, is not strictly speaking the product or effect of the complex of factors which focusses, receives, and reflects it from the fontal Light and Absolute Exemplar, the Divine Word. Only the appearance of the new objects is conditioned by the lens, and the appearance of the new quality by the predisposing complex. The advent of mind was not dissimilar. If God is revealed more fully at one point of the evolutionary sequence than at another, the special manifestation lies in the product, not in the mode of its production. But since mind implies personality, the creative gift here possesses an individual character as opposed to the universal or possibly specific gift of biological life. Given a complex of biological factors produced by the parents, there flashes upon it from the Divine Logos what has been termed a seminal reason, *ratio seminalis,* the informing soul of the new organism, whether the vegetative soul of a plant, the sentient but irrational and mortal soul of a beast, or the rational and immortal soul of a man. The view that new qualities and kinds of being emerge when particular complexities of a lower order have been achieved is known as emergent evolution, and is often stated as though the higher emerged automatically from the complex of lower factors. Thus stated, emergent evolution contradicts the law of causality. But in the light of theism it assumes an altogether different aspect: emergence and creation are seen to be two aspects of the same fact—emergence the phenomenal aspect, the product viewed empirically; creation the noumenal aspect; the production viewed metaphysically.

Looking at evolution from below, we see emergence—from above, creation. Everywhere the phenomenal truth visible to science is the reverse, the obverse the noumenal truth visible to philosophy and religion. Therefore the scientist who, as such, views the evolutionary process phenomenally and from below will see God's creative action nowhere. The metaphysician and theologian who views it noumenally from above will see it everywhere. Evolution thus exemplifies Father Faber's profound observation that God's revelations are also concealments; 'that He discloses Himself by hiding Himself.' [8]

It has always been a commonplace that man is a microcosm whose composition contains inorganic matter, vegetable and animal life, and intelligent spirit. And if it appears that in his ancestry also he is a microcosm, his genealogy corresponding to his present composition, a recapitulation of the evolu-

[8] *The Blessed Sacrament,* p. 362.

tionary process,[4] so that he traces his lineage from inorganic matter through vegetable and animal life to intelligent spirit, the genealogical microcosm does but re-inforce the actual. If man is undeniably matter, vegetable, animal, and spirit, why is it difficult to admit that his evolution has passed through the lower stages which still co-exist in him with the highest? The lower has not produced the higher simply of itself, has not been able of its own power to add to its stature the successive cubits of additional being. Only the Divine Fount and Fullness of Being can thus raise His creature to a higher perfection of essence, involving a new mode and quality of being at every step nearer to Himself, though always infinitely distant. To the religious eye evolution, the gradual development of being, the ascent of degrees, is an objective psalm of degrees, a Gradual Psalm sung to the praise of the Lord and Giver of Life, as Life ascends towards His Temple of Spirit. And in human history this psalmody is continued in a different way, no longer as hitherto wholly objective and necessary, but increasingly a subjective and free worship. 'We glow inwardly

[4] Even the stages of man's embryological development correspond generally, though not in detail, with stages or levels of racial evolution. But I am speaking more widely of man as in his nature a recapitulation of the entire evolutionary process.

and go forward . . . we ascend thy ways and sing a song of degrees. *Inardescimus et imus. Ascendimus ascensiones et cantamus canticum graduum.'* The creative evolutionary process, creation in and through evolution, is thus a hymn of praise—faint in matter, louder in the plant and animal, clear and jubilant in the spirit of man, till it reaches its climax in that eternal anthem of the heavenly choirs, in whose perfect harmony the discordant notes of blind necessity and evil will are for ever silent: 'Holy, Holy, Holy Lord God of Hosts, Heaven and Earth are full of Thy glory. *Sanctus, Sanctus, Sanctus, Dominus Deus Sabaoth. Pleni sunt cæli et terra, gloria, tua.'*

YELLOW

ART

SPECTROSCOPICALLY yellow is composed of green and red. And art is blent of natural life and the spiritual love which is, at least implicitly, religious. Art occupies the frontier between biological and spiritual life. Moreover, art, sex and religion, here symbolised respectively by the yellow, orange and red bands of the rainbow, are the three most intense and concentrated unions with concrete reality, the three pre-eminently ecstatic forms of human experience. And in all three not knowledge but love in one form or another is primary, the intrinsic motive. Wust is justified in regarding the artist (inclusive of the thinker, in so far as he gives verbal expression to his thought), the lover, and the mystic or saint, as the three supreme human types.[1] The three activities are not of course necessarily exclusive. Every man is normally religious. The irreligious man is a mutilated man, and even then religion is still operative in his soul, unrecognised and masked. Sex enters into the life of the vast majority and only

[1] *Catharsis of the Creative Genius.*

a specific religious vocation can compensate for its absence. And every man is an artist. For the artist is not simply the man who practices one of the fine arts—painter, sculptor, musician, dancer, poet, actor —though these are artists *par éminence*. But as Wust has explained,[2] man of his very nature expresses the forms of things, their inner form or significance, in some external shape, be it only verbal. He is thus relatively and secondarily a creator, continuing in his human mode the creative work by which the Divine Word gives external expression to His ideas.

The doctrine that art expresses the 'significant form' of things states its metaphysical essence. Moreover, it is a canon by which to appraise and harmonise the realist and expressionist views of art. The realist is right when he insists that art shows and copies what is objectively present in nature. In this human art differs from the divine, which is pure expressionism. In creating, God copies nothing but Himself.[3]

---

[2] *Dialektik des Geistes*, 154-168, and *Catharsis of the Creative Genius*, passim.

[3] The mediævalist combined with an expressionist theology of divine creation an excessively realist theory of art. Dante's ideal of painting is cinema-photography: *'non vide me' di me, chi vide il vero'* (*Purg.*, x., 34-45, 58-63, 79-81; xii., 64-69, esp. 68). And the child, though his actual art, like that of the early Middle Ages, is extremely expressionist, is in intention a naïve realist.

The expressionist in turn is right when he insists that art is not simply copying, but reflects and expresses the personality of the artist in forms chosen and adapted for that purpose. For the artist's personality largely determines what significant forms he shall see in nature and display, and above all under what aspect he shall see and display them. Art, literary or plastic, does not show us simply what the object is in itself or simply what is the artist's subjective reaction to it, except of course when the latter is itself the direct object. It shows what the artist sees in nature and only secondarily what is equally a fact—his subjective reaction to what he sees. The artist's representation is selection, in which the irrelevancies which in nature obscure the expression of the significant form are eliminated. Hence the work of art expresses the significant form, the idea, of the object better than the object itself.

This formal or ideal theory of art was held by Plotinus; on this point he forsakes the realism of his master Plato, for whom the artefact was but the copy of the material object, the copy of a copy: [a] 'The arts do not directly imitate visible objects, but go back to the rational principles (λόγοι) from which the material object originated. Moreover, the arts

[a] *Republic,* x, 595-600.

supply the defects of objects because they possess beauty', and 'the beauty of art is far greater than any beauty present in the external object.' [5]

In nature the pattern is usually obscured by redundancies and excrescences, defects and distortion, and therefore realised imperfectly and impurely. For in nature, as we have seen, the matter-energy fails at every turn the form imposed upon it, and a disorder of conflicting forces obstructs its embodiment. In the words of Dante:

> 'La cera di costoro e chi la duce
> Non sta d'un modo, e però sotto il segno
> Ideale poi più e men traluce. . . .
> Se fosse a punto la cera dedutta . . .
> La luce del suggel parebbe tutta;
> Ma la natura la dà sempre scema
> Similemente operando all'artista
> Ch'ha l'abito dell' arte e man che trema.'

'The wax of these [contingent things] and that which mouldeth it standeth not in one mode, and therefore 'neath the ideal stamp is more or less transparent. . . . Were the wax exactly moulded . . . the light of the signet would be all apparent; but nature ever furnisheth it faulty, doing as doth the artist who hath the knack [the skill] of the art and a trembling hand.' [6]

[5] *Enneads*, v, 8, 1.
[6] *Parad.*, xiii., 67-69, 73, 75-78. Tr. Okey.

The course of evolution, that is to say of creation through evolution, has been a gradual and interrupted imposition of form on this recalcitrant, because deficient, matter. Man as artist-creator continues the process from the point where this evolutionary creation has left it. He too stamps on a recalcitrant material an 'ideal stamp,' which however he does not invent, but finds in nature already preexistent in the rough. He displays this pattern by cleansing it from the alloy of its encumbered and therefore obscured natural embodiment. Art is the gold, nature the ore whence it is mined.

Art therefore does not simply copy but continues and supplements nature. It is the fulfilment of nature, as grace fulfils it in a higher order, or as love fulfils the law. As the sciences reveal the mechanism of nature's body, art displays it as the living body of a unitary and unifying form, as it were its soul when the object is a living organism, literally the soul.

This is true of art universally, even of the humblest craftsmanship. The sole difference between the arts and the humbler utilitarian crafts is one of proportion between the purpose of practical utility and the display of pattern for its own sake. Hence the difficulty of drawing an exact line of demarcation between the crafts and the fine arts. Instead of or in addition to practical use, didactic purpose may also enter into a work of art. In itself this is not, as is often supposed, injurious to art: of this the Gospels and the *Divina Commedia* are sufficient proof. Indeed of the greatest artists, the majority, in literature at least, have been inspired by a didactic purpose, for example, Plato, Virgil, Dante, Milton, Wordsworth. But neither the utilitarian nor the didactic factor is itself artistic. The strictly artistic quality in a work of art is the display of significant form or pattern. To this therefore the utilitarian or didactic purpose must be strictly subordinate. If it interferes with the display of form the artistic value of the work is correspondingly diminished. There are no doubt occasions when the literary artist, at least, may and should intend primarily a didactic purpose, for example, when he composes works of spirituality, history, and the like. But in so far he is not acting as an artist but as a teacher or historian. From this point of view the historian is in a particularly difficult position. He must be strictly faithful to the facts. But if he is to be more than a mere chronicler or compiler of insignificant details he must display a pattern: as an artist he must treat the landscape of history as the painter treats the physical landscape. But he is then tempted to force events and motives into the mould of his pattern, for pattern is realised in history even less purely perhaps than in nature, since the factors are here more complex. If he is a faithful historian, he is not an artist; if an artist, not a faithful historian. The dilemma cannot be altogether escaped. A sacrifice must be made in both directions, a balance struck. And the perfect balance between the faithful chronicler and the artist, the historical photographer and painter, is no doubt impossible of attainment. Though the historian may not deliberately falsify for art's sake, he must commit himself to general statements, which ignore a host of minor qualifications which would obscure the pattern he is seeking to portray. But the pattern itself must be truly present in the facts. Otherwise the work would not be history but sheer romance. The greatest historians must be content to approximate to the unattainable ideal, shading their portraits as delicately as they can in the light of the fullest possible knowledge of detail. And in practice historians will be roughly divided into supplementary groups, equally indispensable: the historian-chroniclers devoted to the accurate determination of detailed fact, and the historian-artists who display in these facts the pattern they imperfectly embody.[7]

[7] There is also the historian-scientist who interprets the data of history by the data of sociology.

Didactic art can exist only when the idea or system of ideas to be expressed is the significant form, the idea, of the work of art, organising from within the matter it selects, and in which it is embodied. Thus the providence of Roman Imperialism is the organic form of the Æneid, selecting and arranging the material of its own revelation. Similarly, the Catholic scheme of salvation is the idea or significant form of the *Divina Commedia*. If the idea the artist would convey is not thus the form of his work apprehended in his material and its internal and organic principle of life, but is forced upon it from without, as a mould artificially imposed, the work of art is dead: instead of art we have mere didacticism.

Moreover an idea or system of ideas can become the soul or significant form of a co-operative art. The mediæval craftsman had but slight understanding of Catholicism as an organic system of ideas. Nor, presumably, did the masons at work upon the Parthenon consciously understand the ideal which inspired Pericles and Pheidias. But in either case the craftsmen were members of an organic society, inspired respectively by the Catholic and Hellenic ideals, societies of which those ideals were the significant form. As such these ideals became the significant form of their craftsmanship. No individual genius can adequately present an idea without the co-operation of a society inspired and organised by it. Form must call to form. This is the reason why the Gothic revival, for all the devotion and labour it evoked, failed so dismally. Individually Pugin apprehended more clearly perhaps, and no doubt more passionately, than the mediæval mason, the significant form of Gothic architecture; hence his designs are beautiful and satisfying.[8] But his patrons and craftsmen belonged to a society of which the mediæval view of Catholicism was not the organic form. Lacking Pugin's genius they could not escape from that society by a powerful apprehension of the Gothic idea. They could but order or copy mechanically external forms to them lifeless and insignificant. Hence the execution is disappointing—at best clever copying.

Nor indeed was the idea apprehended by Pugin wholly identical with the idea of the mediæval religion and culture. It over-emphasised the ritual aspect, as opposed to the philosophic, of which he probably knew very little. Moreover, as his idealised pictures of the mediæval city prove, it was too abstract and took too little account of concrete realities. Had Pugin been able to return to the fifteenth cen-

[8] Kenneth Clark, *The Gothic Revival,* pp. 170-1.

tury of his dreams, the shock might have killed him. Even for himself the correspondence between idea and expression was insufficient. Ruskin, on the other hand, who saw the necessity for a vital movement in art, for a spiritual ideal socially embodied, and for that reason rightly condemned the Gothic Revival, was unable to find any certain and consistent system of ideas which he could accept and preach. He saw clearly what was wrong. He could not see what and where was the truth. Hence he flung from inconsistency to inconsistency—caught gleams of truth at every turn but was unable to follow them up, and ended in the madness of despair.

And if in literature the dependence of individual apprehension of an ideal form on its communal apprehension is less obvious, it is none the less real. A literary masterpiece of the first rank is possible only when the idea that inspired it has already been apprehended and expressed more imperfectly and obscurely by precursors in the same literary milieu—is, as we say, 'in the air,' and finds a public prepared to understand it. The genius is never a solitary pioneer.

Great art is thus always the individual-social expression of an idea—or rather organic system of ideas—expressed in other media by the religion, speculation and social structure with which it is bound up. And if that ideal form is grossly inadequate, the art which embodies it, though it may be honest, vital, and technically accomplished, must fall short of an art which embodies as organically, and with equal perfection of technique, a more adequate idea.

It may be asked whether this apprehension and display of pattern is not rather a contemplation of the object than a concrete union with it, and whether the artist is not therefore to be grouped rather with the scientist and metaphysician than with the lover and religious man of whose experience concrete and vital union is the predominant factor. The artist is in fact intermediate between both groups. His union with his object is certainly less concrete than that of the lover and religious man. But it is more concrete than that of the scientist and metaphysician. This is shown by the more emotional and vital quality of his apprehension. He enters more into the energy or life of his object as a concrete whole than the savant or philosopher; these are concerned directly with the abstract form, whereas it is in vital union with the concrete life of the object that the artist apprehends the forms he embodies.[9] This, however, is truer of the plastic, pictorial, and musical,

[9] See p. 11.

than of the literary artist, who occupies an intermediate position between the plastic artist and the thinker. At one extreme, as the poet, he is primarily an artist; at the other his art becomes subordinate to intellectual speculation. But in so far as he is an artist his contacts with reality are concrete and vital. Indeed the artist is distingished by his appetite for intense living: he leads, in the words of Keats, 'a life of sensations rather than of thoughts.' He, above all men, will pluck the fruits of experience, will taste life to the full. It is for this reason that he is apt to be impatient of restraint, to be unconventional and bohemian. And—because, as we have seen, the contact of the literary artist with his object is less concrete and vital than the contact of his fellow-artists —sculptors, painters, musicians, dancers, actors are on the whole more unconventional and uncontrolled than men of letters, with the exception of the most purely artistic of all literary types, the lyric poet, and perhaps also the dramatist. Need I say, I am speaking only of tendency; other factors may and do supervene to counteract it.

Hitherto I have spoken somewhat vaguely of the intuition of beauty. What more exactly is this distinctively æsthetic intuition? It is, I believe, the artist's direct and concrete intuition of the form or pattern in objects, more concrete and less distinct than the mathematician's intuition of numerical law, less concrete and more distinct than the psychological intuition of the soul, or the religious intuition of God. It is an intuition of that form or pattern as intrinsically and therefore necessarily invested with an ultimate quality irreducible to anything besides, in fact the specific quality of pattern as thus apprehensible. We term this quality beauty. Beauty has been aptly denominated *splendor formæ*—the resplendence of form or pattern. The description, of course, does not explain it—it is an indefinable ultimate—but it points out its essential dependence on pattern or significant form. And when St. Augustine[10] says that 'beauty consists in the harmony of parts irradiated by a delightful splendour' he is referring to this resplendence of pattern, though the inherent and necessary character of the latter is not brought out. This moreover is the significance of the bond between beauty and truth, on which the schoolmen and writers on æsthetics down to Rodin insist. For truth, the objective truth which is here in question, is fundamentally the significant form, the harmonious pattern, as opposed to irrational and

---

[10] *De Musica*, vi.; quoted by Father E. Künzle, O.F.M. *Ethik und Æsthetik*, p. 24.

insignificant disorder. True, not everyone who apprehends this pattern and its quality is therefore an artist. He may be unable to express his intuition. But he is at least an interior artist. For his apprehension of beauty must take shape in his own mind, must express itself in some mental image, a *verbum mentale æstheticum.*[11] But it is only when expressed in some external medium, be it simply verbal, that interior pattern becomes clear; and the degree of the clarity will depend on the percipient's power of artistic expression.

If beauty is thus inherently bound up with pattern why are there ugly patterns? An ugly pattern is one in which the inner pattern, the significant form or idea, is defectively expressed, distorted and obscured by disorder and formlessness. This no doubt is a matter of degree. But the beauty of creatures, like all their other qualities, is a matter of degree. It is never perfect, but never wholly wanting.

Is it too fanciful to find, in the specific types of creative art, human counterparts and continuations of various aspects of God's creative art in nature? The architect represents in his construction the divine architecture whose foundations are laid in the abyss of blind forces and elements, whose edifice rises to

[11] This point has been well brought out by Croce.

the heaven, where matter and spirit form the temple
of God's unveiled Presence. The sculptor, fashion-
ing his material to the expression of ideal humanity,
copies the work of the Spirit moulding man, soul
and body, to the perfect likeness and image of God,
the archetype eternally present in the Divine Mind.
In line and colour the painter reflects the pattern
and light that by God's creative fiat gradually overcome the disorder, and dispel the darkness of that
chaotic and tenebrous abyss which borders on nothingness, as the pattern and splendour of His Wisdom
are painted on the canvas of time and space. The
composer weaves snatches of the harmony of creation, here marred by discord, but perfect and full in
the consummation of God's work. The dancer in
the melody of rhythmic motion follows that dance
of which Plotinus,[12] Dionysius,[13] Wust,[14] and Mech-
tild of Magdeburg[15] have spoken, the dance of created spirits around the fixed Pole of Being, whose
material images are the revolutions of electrons and
stars, the dance constituted by the double motion of
approach and withdrawal, union and contemplation,

[12] *Enneads,* 6, 9; *cf.* 4, 4, 33-45—the cosmic dance of the
universe.
[13] *Divine Names,* 4, 8. Since the pseudonymity of the Dio-
nysian writings is generally accepted, there seems no need to continue the ugly label 'pseudo.'
[14] *Dialektik des Geistes,* p. 429.
[15] *Fliessende Licht der Gottheit.,* i., 44.

around the Immanent and the Transcendent, the Bridegroom and the King. The poet translates into human language and metre the divine poem of creation and its history. The dramatist tells of the tragedy arising from the conflict between good and evil, disorder and form, as seen in its process by a vision too shortsighted to behold the end. For religion resolves tragedy in triumph, and leaves only the epic of understanding and the lyric of praise. The story of the Cross, for all its suffering and defeat, is no longer a tragedy when the Resurrection is known to be its sequel. Dr. Albert Schweitzer's account of Christ's life is tragedy, a heroic failure ending in despair; the Gospel, as the very word implies, is not. Great tragedy arises only where, though the presence or living memory of a great religious tradition solicits the soul with desire for God, and keeps in view the depths of the human spirit with its capacity and need of the infinite, that tradition has been rejected or so seriously questioned that a more or less conscious agnosticism prevails, at least among the intelligentsia. Instances of this are the Greek Tragedy of the fifth century B.C., contemporary with the rise of rationalist speculation, the age of the Sophists; Elizabethan tragedy, between the Reformation and the secure establishment of Protestant "orthodoxy"; and Scandivinian and Russian tragedy of the last century, when the respective supremacies of Protestantism and Orthodoxy were first seriously shaken by modern rationalism in these outlying provinces of European culture. In every case a sufficient presence of religion to make man conscious of his greatness and dimly aware of his supernatural destiny, a sufficient absence to make his defeat by the evil forces of his environment, mistakes of the good, blunders of folly, defects of temperament, and malicious wills, an insoluble and acutely painful enigma. The soul is perceived to be greater than fate, blind necessity, the 'stars', which nevertheless prevail.[16] And even so the greatest tragedies introduce a lyric element of unformulated consolation and peaceful beauty, in witness of a hope, a victory beyond the tragedian's ken. Shakespeare's tragedies hint an ultimate reconciliation beyond their explicit scope.[17] This is expressed in part by concluding passages of even pitch and calmer tone and in some instances by a lyric note or an utterance of spiritual triumph.[18] And the chorus of Greek tragedies fulfils the same office.

Thus in the fulness of æsthetic vision, at the point

[16] The ἀνάγκη of Greek tragedy corresponds to the 'stars' of Elizabethan.

[17] R. Bradley, *Shakespearian Tragedy,* pp. 36, 84, 147-8, 174, 198, 242, 243-6.

[18] E.g., *Hamlet* (see Bradley, S. T., pp. 147, 174), *Coriolanus,* and from another aspect *Othello, Anthony and Cleopatra.*

where art touches religion, tragedy gives place to a Divine Comedy, and suffering issues in a peace and joy which transfigure it. Art is indeed a transfiguration of the real in the light of the ideal, of nature in the light of spirit. It is the Tabor where nature is seen transfigured by the glory of the immanent Word. It is not the spirit's final resting-place. Though it is 'good for us to be here,' we must descend and travel further. In the supernatural zone of religion, not in the natural zone of art, lies the Mount of Ascension from which the soul rises to the transcendent Word, beyond the images which nature mirrors and art displays. And though in the service and superior light of religion art may embody supernatural truths, it cannot penetrate to the inmost sanctuary where all created forms are left behind. But if it cannot conduct to its goal the will's restless search, it provides a resting-place on the way, where for the moment desire has yielded to fruition, action to contemplation. If in the house of art Mary does not sit at the feet of the Word, Rachel beholds His image. We might almost call art a natural religion of immanence, prelude and antechamber of the supernatural religion of transcendence. And the artist, nature's priest, does on his lower plane what the liturgical priest does on the higher. Both are to offer a sacrifice of praise, respectively natural and supernatural. The rubric bids the priest at the opening of the Canon spread out, raise and join his hands, lifting his eyes to heaven to drop them immediately to the altar in a profound reverence. The artist also spreads out his hands to embrace the whole of nature, sub-human and human, in a generous and universal acceptance and love, then raises hands and eyes in aspiration to that higher World of Spirit whence its patterns derive. He joins his hands in a deep concentration of thought and feeling as though to draw the outer world into his personal experience. At the same time he lowers his eyes by a profound glance into his own spirit, to attain those rich creative depths whence his intuition proceeds. No doubt the minor artist does this but remissly and more superficially. Only the great artist carries out the operation with the power and profundity it demands. That is why he is a great, the former a minor, artist. But it is everywhere the ritual and movement of art.

'But this comprehensive glance must include the evil in the world.' Certainly. Since art sees and displays the significant pattern, it sees the evil, that is the defective and the disordered, integrated and completed by a transcendent harmony, sees it as the foil of good. Art in its theoretical and comparatively external fashion faces evil and overcomes it.[19] For this reason art cannot be evil, though in a concrete instance evil may be united with art.[20] The artist's vision may indeed be largely, though never completely, blind to the higher order of spirit. His sight may be dim for anything which transcends the biological level. But what he sees is good and implies, though the artist fails to recognise it, a spiritual reality beyond. If such art is limited in its range, within that range it may reach a high achievement. It can harm only those whose vision is similarly restricted. Seen in a wider context, with its profounder implications perceived, even a purely naturalist,[21] or as it is often miscalled realist, art can be usefully employed as a hewer of wood and drawer of water in the temple of the Lord. And it will reveal, perhaps more forcibly than any other art, the essential insufficiency of nature to the demands of the human spirit.

Amongst sculptors, Epstein, and amongst writers, Aldous Huxley, are examples of this biological and naturalist outlook. What more cogent exposure than

[19] Wust, *Catharsis of the Creative Genius.*
[20] For the intrinsic and inevitable morality of poetry see Henri Brémond, *Prayer and Poetry* (E.T., pp. 165 *seq.*).
[21] Naturalist as opposed to and excluding the spiritual. As we have seen, art is *as such* natural, not supernatural—however it may serve the supernatural.

Epstein's *Rima* of the romantic fallacy which, mistaking analogy for identity, shadow for substance, invests nature with spiritual values which she reflects but does not possess? No wonder our nature-worshippers and sentimentalists detest it; it is the medicine of which they are badly in need. The despair of Hardy's novels teaches the same lesson in another medium. Like wisdom, art 'is justified of all her children,' and it is her mission to establish this universalism.

ORANGE

SEX

THAT natural life in its fullest, most intense and highest manifestation, love between the sexes, should be placed here above the yellow of art and next to the supreme red of religion may seem surprising, to some even shocking. Is not sex the flower of the biological life in man, where he is closest linked with vegetable and animal life? As biological must it not take rank below art, which is a distinctively intellectual and human activity? From one point of view, yes. If sex were simply the culmination of biological life it would rank below art. Since, however, man has but one soul, at the very point where his biological life burns most fiercely there is kindled a love which, whether he recognises it or not, aspires above the biological level towards the highest plane of spirit, like a flame which, fed on the fuel of earth, rises towards the sky. Moreover this sexual culmination of biological union with natural life and consequent procreation of that life, is the best reflection on the natural plane of the spiritual union and fecundity in which the spiritual life culminates. Sex is therefore aptly symbolised by orange, the colour intermediate between the red of supernatural love, of which it is the image, and yellow, the artist's intuition of beauty.

There is surely no department of human life where common sense and a sane application of metaphysical principles are so necessary as in this sphere of sex. Alternately sex becomes the object of aversion and unbalanced preoccupation. The Victorians pretended it did not exist. To-day the pendulum has swung far in the opposite direction. For many of our contemporaries, particularly among writers, sex would seem to be the most important feature in human life, if not its sole good and purpose. Never before have its phenomena been studied so zealously, scrutinised so closely; never before has the detail of sexual experience—physiological and psychological—been chronicled so minutely and discussed so widely. And this in no spirit of Rabelaisian humour, but with such earnest purpose as in other days and circles has inspired the chroniclers and students of the spiritual life. This reaction from the Victorian lie is nothing portentous or surprising. Man advances by a series of one-sided and excessive movements in different directions. In itself there cannot be too much of a good thing, and sex emphatically is a good, not an evil thing. There can, however, be too much of a good thing relatively to a whole comprising other things as good and better. In this field, as elsewhere, evil lies not in the good affirmed but in the good implicitly or explicitly denied. If the biological life is not the highest human life and if the metabiological love that makes its appearance in sex is not and cannot be at rest in this biological sphere, we cannot be content, like so many of our contemporaries, to keep our eyes fixed so closely on sex that they are blind to other values. Least of all can we be blind to the antitype of which sex is the type, to the spiritual substance of which it is the biological shadow, to the fulfilment of the promise it cannot keep.

Here, however, we are met by the school of Freudian psycho-analysts and their compeers, who tell us that sex is the substance, religion the shadow, that the union of the spirit with God as described by the mystic, with its ecstatic delights, is but a projection of unsatisfied sexuality onto another plane. Their thesis is an example at this critical point of the positivism for which the spiritual is but a shadow and by-product of the physical, and man but the highest achievement of biological life, the King of Animals. The entire scope of this essay has been to maintain the reverse, the true order of material, biological and spiritual being, as it ascends towards the Absolute Being of the Supreme Spirit. We must therefore face this attack and face it frankly.

First for the facts. After religious, sexual experience can undoubtedly be the most intense and ecstatic of all forms of human experience; the witness is convincing. Further—as is shown by the lives of such saints as Augustine, Blessed Ramon Lull and Blessed Angela of Foligno—capacity for powerful sexual experience often accompanies the capacity for intense experience of divine love, and even mystics who from infancy have lived only in the spirit often display a highly sexed temperament. The conclusion is inevitable that a strong susceptibility to sex, a passionate sexuality, is a very favourable predisposition for mystical spirituality.

Moreover, the psychological experiences which accompany sex show a remarkable correspondence with those which accompany mystical prayer. I need but quote the following from that great literary exponent of sexual psychology, the late D. H. Lawrence. He writes as follows: 'She received the maximum of unspeakable communication in touch, dark, subtle, positively silent, a magnificent gift and give again, a perfect acceptance and yielding, a mystery, the reality of that which can never be known, vital, sensual reality that can never be transmuted into mind-content, but remains outside, living body of darkness and silence and subtlety, the mystic body of reality . . . the immemorial magnificence of mystic, palpable, real otherness.' [1] The abyss of sense seems here to mimic the mountain-top of spirit. Substitute 'spiritual' for 'sensual' in this description, and by 'vital' understand not biological but spiritual life, and it corresponds almost verbally to a description of the highest form of mystical prayer from the pen of St. John of the Cross. 'This *touch*,' he writes, 'is a substantial touch of the substance of God in the substance of the soul. Whence the *subtlety* of the delight felt in this is *impossible to describe*. . . . There are no words by which we can designate or explain the deep things of God which take place in such souls. The proper way to speak of them is to feel them, enjoy them, and be *silent*. The touch savours of eternal *life*. . . . Moreover, from the good things the soul enjoys, the unction of the Spirit at times overflows into the body and delights the

---

[1] *Women in Love;* quoted by J. Middleton Murry, *Son of Woman*, p. 117.

entire sensitive nature.' [2] Everything is here but the darkness, and of this the Saint speaks at length elsewhere.

What shall we reply to all this? Are we to surrender our entire position, and admit that the supreme consummation of spirit is an illusory reflection of the biological? A few simple considerations will restore the right perspective.

As we have already insisted, there is but one soul in man, therefore but one psychical energy that is the substratum and matter of all its activities. The difference between them lies not in the energy but in the form imposed upon it, the purpose for which it is employed, the direction in which it is turned. A man or woman of low vitality, and therefore little capacity for intense feeling of any kind, will not normally receive from religion an increase of vital energy. Religion, like any other form of activity, will simply give that energy, such as it is, a particular direction and mode. The same is true of sex. Sexuality is not, as the Freudian maintains, the substratum and energy underlying and feeding all human activities and modes of experience. It is but the flower and supreme biological manifestation of a vital energy not in itself distinctively sexual, but

[2] *Living Flame of Love,* stanza 2.

indeterminate, a matter able to receive a variety of forms, biological or spiritual, natural or supernatural. This is the profound significance and wisdom of the law, superficially paradoxical, which debars eunuchs from the priesthood. Professor Spearman's researches have shown that this is the case with man's intellectual activity. The quantum of energy employed is physiologically fixed, its direction determined by rational choice and logical sequence.[8] When sex and religious devotion seem nevertheless to intensify the quantum of vital energy, they only do so by focussing it at one point more completely than other human activities normally do. Thus the spiritual activity of the soul in prayer differs from its biological activity in sex, not by its matter, the vital energy employed, but by the form imposed upon it.

Whenever the soul thus focusses its activity in a concrete experience, that experience necessarily exceeds the analysis of conceptual ratiocination. This is true of every sensation and intuition, but becomes strikingly evident only when the experience in question is particularly rich and absorbing. The experience that results from intense intellectual or æsthetic

[8] *The Nature of 'Intelligence,'* Ch. ix (pp. 129-141, especially p. 131).

contemplation also displays in its consummation the transcendence of conceptual intelligibility, the contact, silence, subtlety and vitality, common to religious experience and sex. But not only is it less common in this intense degree of concentration, but since the union with the object is, as we have seen, less concrete and more remote than in sexual and religious experience these qualities will not be displayed to the same degree either by intellectual intuition, which presses for conceptual translation, or æsthetic, which presses to be translated into images or verbal symbols.

It is quite untrue that the Saints have been men and women who have sought in religion a substitute for sexual satisfaction withheld. Many did actually experience sex to the full before they turned wholly to God. Others obviously could have experienced it had they wished. There is no doubt a host of people who do seek in religion a substitute for sex, a compensation for natural frustration. But these are not the Saints and mystics, and their shoddy substitute-piety—*Ersatzgeschlecht,* and therefore *Ersatzreligion* —is but a parody of the genuine.

Further, even the psychological qualities or values apparently common to sex and mystical religion are not really identical in both. In the former they are but analogies and images of their counterparts in the latter. The contours of the reflection correspond with those of the object reflected, but they are only reflected contours. Point for point, sexual union, the biological shadow of the spiritual and supernatural union of mystical prayer, reflects that union; but it is simply a reflection, a shadow. Where, as in the descriptions of Lawrence, it seems in its supreme ecstasy to be more than this, we have good reason to suspect an illusion, a psychological projection, the reverse of that by which the Freudian psycho-analyst would explain away the experience of the mystics. Mystical religion is not suppressed and disguised sex, but sex is here in part suppressed and disguised religion.[4] Lawrence was obviously a man of the most profound religious capacity and need. The solvent effect of modern rationalism upon the emotional pietism of his childhood left that need and capacity unfulfilled. With the fiery passion of a mighty spirit, goaded moreover by a losing battle with physical disease, this Augustine *manqué* threw himself into sex. Life concrete and intense he must have at all costs. Of the supernatural life he was

---

[4] This is not to deny the indubitable occurrence of the counter-illusion, suppressed sex masquerading as religion. It is only to be expected. For the subject of sex and religion is the same, the human composition of soul and body.

ignorant. There remained only its shadow, biological life. Into this he therefore plunged headlong
and desperate, and, of course, at the point where it
burns with keenest flame, where its current runs
most strongly. Reason, the idol of his contemporaries—his education, be it remembered, belonged
to the nineteenth century—was to him dead and
deadly, as in isolation it is, being but the instrument
of life. God seemed an outgrown myth. The only
life-giving spirit within his ken was the immanent
spirit of biological life and love. But all the while
his soul in virtue of its very nature penetrated beyond that biological zone and in its hidden centre
was in actual contact with God. He therefore by
the *tour de force* of a perverted genius read into
the life of sex obscure needs and experiences, half-
conscious and misinterpreted, of this metabiological
abyss within himself, that dark ground of which
Ruysbroeck has so much to say, where God dwells
by nature in the human spirit. But the biological
experience of sex could not respond to the metabiological demand, could not give what he would fain
find in it, because it was not and could not be *there*.
It could indeed give him the shadow, the analogue,
of mystical prayer, thereby encouraging him to persist in his vain quest. But the shadow necessarily

slipped from his eager grasp. He never got what he wanted; merely a semblance, in itself good, but infinitely too little for his spirit's need. Hence perpetual disillusion, restless, never satisfied search, hate and despair. He will end by hating women, because they are women, not God. To what extent in his accounts of temporary fruition he imagined a fulfilment which God alone could have given, to what extent the passing image of that fulfilment was invested with the quality which he dimly felt must attach to the satisfaction of man's desire, we cannot with any certainty determine. But his tragedy proclaims to all who have ears to hear that the illusion lies not with those who regard spiritual union with God as man's highest, noblest and truest life, but with those for whom the biological life is the sole reality and its sexual flower man's *summum bonum*.

And here Lawrence the genius, like other geniuses, is representative of an active movement of thought and feeling among more ordinary men. He is the spokesman of all those who to-day, more or less consciously, make sex a religion. Rationalism has robbed them of faith in God and the spiritual love-life of union with Him. Being men, not calculating-machines or vegetables, they must have life concrete, intense, passionate. They therefore turn to sex, the biological image of spiritual life, its passion and union—not for what it really can give and has given in all ages, but for the content of that other and supreme love-life which it reflects. They are, of course, disappointed, and they will continue to be disappointed. But their search is a judgment, a testimony and a summons. It is in the first place a judgment. Sex thus illegitimately idolised is the whale that devours Jonah as he seeks to escape by flight to Tarshish the task which Jahweh has laid upon him. Man, whose very nature as a spirit bids him find his end in union with God, has attempted in the modern Enlightenment to find it in a purely 'rational' and secular order of life, aptly symbolised by Tarshish, Tartessus, at the dawn of antiquity the great commercial emporium of the Mediterranean-Atlantic trade route. The tempest arises, war, economic stress or revolution, his frail craft founders. Human ratiocination cannot attain the clear and complete system of truths on which alone a stable world-order of a purely rational description could be constructed. He is devoured by the submarine monster of biological life lurking in his irrational instincts, the whale of sex. For, like the whale, sex should feed man's wants, not swallow him. But the sea-monster may after all prove an instrument of his deliverance. In its belly, dark and confined, he learns, like the prophet, the impotence of his natural powers to satisfy the demands of his spirit, his need of divine illumination and grace. Thus the judgment of sex in its modern idolatry becomes a testimony to man's need of the life and love which God alone can bestow, a witness to the reality it prefigures and reflects.

There remains the summons. It is not simply a reaction from Victorian self-deception which has determined the modern cult of sex. It is, as we have seen in the case of its prophet D. H. Lawrence, an attempt to make sex the substitute for loss of religion —to find the substance in the shadow, the light in its reflection. All who understand this must see in this worship of sex a summons to make the truth known to these seekers, to show them where alone their satisfaction lies, the treasure for which they are looking in the wrong place. They are more likely to be convinced than their fathers, idolaters of abstract reason and utilitarians of commercial interest, men who could degrade religion itself into the patronised guardian of respectability, property, and the *status quo*. When once the right ontological order is apprehended, sex will take its proper place and appear in its true perspective, to be surrendered by a minority for a particularly close union with God in which the biological energies will be concentrated to the utmost in the service of the spirit, by the vast majority accepted for what it is and no more, the highest biological good in which the fire of vital life and love is focussed to its utmost concentration, and as such the image and indicator of that supernatural love-life whose intrinsic solicitation of the human spirit makes it impossible for man to find his final satisfaction in sexuality, and kindles at the apex of biological sex an aspiration of spiritual love whose proper object and fulfilment lies in a higher order, being nothing less than God Himself.

That sex thus reflects and points to religion is also attested by the nature-religions, whose mysteries often culminate in some kind of sexual symbolism or ceremonial, not from any depravity of man's heart, but because although, unlike the modern neo-pagan, their adherents recognise a distinctively religious reality, they cannot disentangle it from the biological sphere and its sexual fulfilment, vegetable, animal and human. Such ceremonial, which often took the form of a sacred marriage, ἱερὸς γάμος, between the mother-goddess of earth's fertility and a vegetation- or sky-god,[5] points to its anti-type, the wedlock between nature, represented by the human microcosm, and God.

[5] *E.g.,* In the cults of Hadad-Atargatis, Tammuz-Ishtar, Sabazios-Attis-Cybele, and most probably the Eleusinian mysteries.

The Catholic liturgy contains a rite which, with the delicacy and pure beauty befitting the cult of the spirit, represents the antitypal nuptials,[6] the ἱερὸς γάμος which these crude ceremonials of nature-worship foreshadowed. It is the solemn symbolism with which the font is blessed on Holy Saturday and the Eve of Pentecost. The Paschal Candle, which symbolises Christ, Giver of the Divine Life from Heaven—its flame the Word, its wick and wax His soul and body—is plunged into the font, the watery womb of natural life, subject-matter of the supernatural form to be imposed upon it. Thrice, ever deeper, it is plunged into the water, as though to penetrate with its impregnation of supernatural life—'*arcana sui Numinis admixtione fecundet*'—every level of created being as it enters into the composition of man, his intellect, his biological life, his very flesh—or, if you prefer, his intuition, reasoning and sensation.

Thus is introduced into that fontal womb the fecundating power—'*fecundet*'—of the creative Spirit, '*descendat in hanc plenitudinem fontis virtus*

---

[6] Whereas the pagan rituals insist on the external and accidental factors of sex due to its physiological nature, Christian symbolism has everywhere seized the central significance in which it reflects and represents a higher union. This is presumably the reason why Catholicism, while freely admitting erotic symbolism in her religious literature, has, unlike the Indian religions, excluded it from her painting and plastic art.

Spiritus Sancti,' that so made fertile of a divine life
—'*sanctificatione concepta*'—it, or the deified nature
it represents, in a word grace, may bring forth a
humanity already deified in potency and promise by
the Spirit of our Father indwelling and informing
it. In the accomplishment of this mystery the ultimate significance of natural sex and procreation is
revealed, the supernatural wedlock and fertility of
which they are shadow, symbol and prophecy.

The moderns are justifiably disgusted with romanticism; they rightly feel it to be false and therefore
sentimental. Sentimentalism is sentiment divorced
from truth. But they cannot perceive the reason of
that falsity; they imagine the sole error of romanticism is the refusal to recognise adequately the biological character of sex. It is deeper than that, re-
joining fundamentally the error of its modern opponents, who while fully recognising the biological
quality of sex idolise it nevertheless. For the cardinal
error of romanticism was to invest sex, indeed natural life in general, with a spiritual value derived
from elsewhere and there alone justified and due.
Where the moderns ascribe an absolute value to the
admittedly biological, the romantics pretended that
the biological is the spiritual. A metaphysic such as
that implicit in Christian theism will not invest the

biological with the qualities of spirit. Its adherents will be realists, not romantics, in their attitude to sex. The romantic view of sex is a bastard growth, an illegitimate blend of Christian idealism and biological naturalism, in fact, like romanticism generally, a masquerade of biological values in idealist garb.[7] As such its heart and inspiration is that 'lie in the soul' which Plato so severely condemns. It is due to this fundamental lie that the final artistic product of romanticism, Pre-Raphaelite art, for all its fidelity to the externals of nature, is essentially false. To realise this falsity of romantic love we have only to remember the grotesque self-deception with which Shelley tried to represent to himself and others his sexual relationships as spiritual and ideal loves.[8] How tonic by comparison the honesty of Byron!

Lawrence's attitude was very different. He—in this, as we have seen, representative of his contemporaries—read into the avowedly biological the

[7] See Christopher Dawson, *Christianity and Sex,* p. 32.

[8] No doubt Shelley, like the other great romantics, transcended in his best work the romantic fallacy. Shelley hymns intellectual beauty; Wordsworth tells of the 'soul that is the eternity of thought'; Coleridge was a student of Neo-Platonism; Keats beholds a beauty not of flesh. But they were unable to attain a clear and consistent transcendentalism. The romantic confusion between biological and metabiological values obscured their vision to the end. Even Wordsworth's final orthodoxy was external—a refuge of disillusionment, without organic connection with the nature-mysticism that inspired his genuine poetry.

value of the religious and spiritual. He did not
attempt to persuade himself that the biological was
not biological but ideal and spiritual. To expect the
physiological to yield the value of spirit is an error;
to pretend like Shelley that the physiological is spiritual is self-deception. And error is easier removed.
But this confusion and false witness of romantic love
unconsciously testifies to that sphere where the sublime love of spirits is at home, the supernatural
sphere of God and the communion of souls in Him.
If platonic love, to use an accepted but gross mis-
nomer, is absurd, unnatural and empty, if romantic
love is misconceived and the modern cult of sex mis-
placed, all are distortions of that true love of the
spirit, of which sexual love is the biological image,
the love of God, and in God of our fellows both
generally and in particular.

Merely natural virginity is barren, a veritable contradiction in terms. Artemis is a sterile and bastard
figure between Aphrodite, the mother of natural,
and Mary, the mother of supernatural life.[9] But
there is, as Professor Hildebrand has pointed out, a
specific love between individuals in God. This love
in God may be between friends of the same sex, but

[9] Cf. Plotinus' distinction between Aphrodite Pandemos, sexual
love, and Aphrodite Urania, the love of God. *Enneads,* vi, 9, 9.

it may also unite a man and a woman. In this case, owing to the psychological differences between the sexes, it will necessarily possess a distinctive quality. But even then it is altogether above the sphere of sex as a biological function. Here, and here alone, we find that spiritual love between man and woman to which Shelley's romantic amours falsely laid claim. Such were the ties that united St. Francis with St. Clare, St. Francis of Sales with St. Jane Chantal. In this highest personal union with creatures the sphere of nature and its physiological life has been transcended. This love—friendship is altogether too cold a term—is union in God, for God, and with God. Biological sex lies below us; the orange has passed into red.

RED

RELIGION

La gloria di Colui che tutto move
Per l'universo penetra e risplende
In una parte più, e meno altrove.

'THE glory of Him who moveth all penetrates the universe and shines in one part more, in another less.' [1] In all human experience the light of God shines. Nowhere is there total darkness. But in unequal measure. There is a supreme zone bathed in the light of the Divine Sun, though the luminary is never visible on earth. To that zone we have now mounted. By the double ascent of speculation and concrete union we have climbed the ladder of being to the summit where contemplation and vital union are most closely united, namely, religion. When St. Bonaventure was about to compose his guide-book of the spirit through the graded ranks of created being to the Creator, he retired to Mount Alvernia, that Christian Sinai where God had appeared to St.

---

[1] *Paradiso*, 1, 1-3.

Francis, not, as to Moses on the older Horeb, to engrave a law of fear and death with letters on stones, but to write the law of love and life with wounds, in the Saint's living flesh, pierced by the delicious pain of ecstasy. There he sought, as he tells us, to taste that ecstatic peace which his master had proclaimed and in which he placed man's wisdom, satisfaction and happiness. Ecstasy and peace in one, this is indeed the perfect experience for which man's heart is athirst. Without ecstasy, intense life, he is no better than a vegetable, without peace he is distracted and dissatisfied. Ecstasy satisfies his need of concrete and vital union, peace his need of contemplation. The contemplation of metaphysics, the blue of God's bow, gives peace but little ecstasy; the contemplative union of art, its yellow, gives ecstasy and peace but more superficially; sex, the orange, in its fulfilment, ecstasy but little peace: and in all these the ecstasy and the peace are deficient and transitory. Religious experience, the red band of Divine Love, particularly in its supreme mode, the experience of supernatural prayer, is peace and ecstasy in one, 'the ecstatic peace' for which the soul 'pants,' [2] those 'ecstatic excesses of Christian

[2] *Itinerarium Mentis ad Deum,* Prol. 1; quoted, Gilson, *Phil. de S. Bonaventure,* p. 76.

wisdom'[8] which do not disappoint or fail, but are perfect and eternal fulfilment.

Religious experience, however, is suspect language with many. They understand by its subjectivism, the exaltation of emotion above reason, the individualism that rejects institutional religion, the false spiritualism which would dispense with visible embodiments of religion such as public worship, sacraments, and ceremonies, as indifferent, if not actually mischievous. And in particular its critics associate with religious experience the pantheist immanentism—in truth religion's most deadly and insidious foe—which finds the object of religion in the religious experience itself, in the subject's spiritual life, or more generally in the created universe experienced religiously as divine, and will admit no transcendent Creator, wholly other than the world or the human soul which experiences His presence and action.

Who would deny that religious experience has been, and often is, so misinterpreted? But if, in defiance of the adage, abuse is good reason to reject what is abused, we should be obliged to reject every form of experience. And we should be particularly obliged to reject those higher and richer and more

[8] *Itinerarium Mentis ad Deum,* Prol. 3; quoted, Gilson, *Phil de S. Bonaventure,* p. 77.

intense forms of experience which, just because they engage their subject most deeply, are peculiarly disastrous when abused and pre-eminently liable to abuse. Above all we should be obliged to reject religion *en bloc*. For here more than anywhere else the abuse is most extensive and most deadly. Its absolute claim and the essential obscurity of its transcendent object have combined to render religion—received, as it must be, by human subjects, ignorant, stupid, or even malevolent—the field most fertile in curses as well as blessings to mankind. In the richest soil weeds flourish most luxuriantly. To enumerate the abuses of religion would be to labour a commonplace. We know them only too well. The rise of European rationalism in the Enlightenment succeeded an epoch which, while particularly fertile in the highest forms of religious life—it was indeed pre-eminently the age of the mystics—was also distinguished by religious warfare and persecution, controversy and hate, which for some two centuries devastated Europe physically and intellectually in the name and intended service of religion. The Encyclopædists followed the Dragonnades.

Are we therefore with the rationalists to reject religion because of these abuses, which, regarded in the right light, rather witness to its truth and supreme value? *Corruptio optimi pessima.* If not, why denounce religious experience because of the abuses mentioned above? And when we read of neuropathic perversions or concomitants of religious experience, we shall do well to remember the morbidities, hysteria and perversions which abound in the sexual sphere, the appalling and disgusting record of sexual pathology. If sex is nevertheless normal, healthy and good, a union with and apprehension of objective reality, how illogical to reject religious experience as subjective illusion, when in power, satisfaction and delight, and in its value, intellectual and spiritual, it incalculably exceeds any other form of human experience.

But what precisely do we mean by religious experience? In the widest sense it is synonymous with religion. Everything known is as such experienced. What is meant, however, by the term is experience of a distinctive and immediate religious quality, direct apprehension of a religious object, truth or value. That is to say, it is an ultimate experience which, since it is not sensation, must be amongst those spiritual intuitions which apprehend all ultimates not apprehended by the senses.

No more than any other form of ultimate intuition is religious experience exclusively or primarily subjective. Naturally a subjective factor enters into it as into all human experience. And since its object, God, is particularly present in the depths of the soul, the most spiritual creation of which we have direct knowledge, it is as there present and operative that He is pre-eminently apprehended. This, however, involves a special prominence of the subjective factor. Further, since in His absolute transcendence God is necessarily the most obscure of all objects of human knowledge, religious experience must be the most obscure of all forms of experience, and its conceptual formulation the most inadequate. Another door open to subjectivism. But all this cannot destroy its essential objective and transcendent reference. And not only does it present an object external to the experient, it also presents an object external to the universe—an absolute transcendence and otherness. Immanentism contradicts the essence of the experience it claims to interpret—the apprehension, however dim, of an Absolute in contrast with the contingency of creatures including the soul itself. Religious experience is essentially a reception of God's self-manifestation, that is to say, His self-revelation, though normally without any distinct communication of religious doctrine not previously known.

Nor is it emotion. Most commonly, no doubt, it is coloured, more or less strongly, by emotion. All the more intense and profounder forms of human experience, sexual, artistic, metaphysical, are normally invested with emotion. They are the experiences of an embodied spirit, and a spiritual emotion would seem to accompany even the supreme experience of mystical prayer, in which sensible devotion has been left behind. But the emotion is not therefore the intuition. Otherwise the two could not be, as they often are, divorced. The dry experience of certain souls or periods of spiritual growth proves that the inhibition of emotion is not the absence of apprehension.

Nor yet are the immediate and ultimate apprehensions of the intellect, whether the more abstract and metaphysical or the more concrete and religious, more irrational than the mediate operations of the discursive reason. On the contrary, they are a more synthetic, fundamental and concrete operation of the intellect. For if metaphysical intuition is more abstract than religious, it is more concrete than discursive ratiocination. The contrary belief is merely a prejudice in favour of the clearer but more abstract and analytic forms of knowledge as against the more obscure but more concrete and synthetic forms. And

that prejudice in turn is the counterpart and continuation of the prejudice in favour of sensible knowledge and its physical data, as against intellectual
knowledge and its mental data.

Moreover the data of religious experience are no
more to be simply accepted in the raw, unco-ordi-
nated and uncontrolled, than the data of sensation
or of other forms of intellectual intuition. Like these
they must be harmonised, related to the rest of experience, and integrated in the entire body of knowledge—that is to say, interpreted and set in order,
and thus controlled by the discursive reason: 'policed'
by it, as Wust observes.⁴ Not the acceptance of
religious experience, but the failure to submit it to
this interpretation and control has led to the fanati-
cism and folly which have done so much to discredit
not only religious experience but religion in general.
Not indeed that discursive reason controls its data
or indeed the data of intuition in any form by pro-
nouncing on their validity. For these data are its
own starting-points, postulates and presuppositions.
But it controls them by analysing and explaining
their content. It interprets the scriptures of sensation
and intuition.

Nor yet is religious experience purely individual.

⁴ *Dialektik des Geistes, pp.* 296-8.

The experience of the individual would remain a mere potency or abortive growth, unawakened or unrecognised, without external religious teaching. And at best its content is utterly inadequate. No artist, not even an artist of genius, confines his artistic knowledge to the product of his own æsthetic insight. He studies the work of other artists, which shows him what they have seen and he would not otherwise have seen for himself. How absurd, then, for even a man of exceptional religious endowment and insight to confine his religious knowledge to his own experience! He must accept the testimony of those great masters of religion, the Saints, to whom God has pre-eminently revealed Himself, and in particular those teachers of His public revelation to whom He has communicated religious truth else hidden, and he must also hear the witness of the society to whose keeping God has entrusted this deposit of religious truth for the universal instruction of mankind. The acceptance of religious experience therefore, far from excluding faith in God's revelation to and through others, involves the acceptance of such revelation in so far as it is made known to us.

But it must, of course, be a vital and personal acceptance, not a mere external and notional credence. As the artist must re-apprehend the æsthetic insights of his predecessors, the religious man must re-apprehend the religious insights he accepts, must in a secondary sense relive them, and incorporate them by a vital assimilation into his religious life. A description of mystical experience, a doctrine or ritual which has been born of religious insight, and embodies it objectively—that insight being in another aspect a self-revelation of God—is dead until it has thus been vitally accepted and relived by the experience of the believer. He need not, indeed he cannot, re-experience the original insight as such. But he must experience it as reflected and embodied in the description, doctrine or ceremony. Moreover the degree of this re-apprehension and vital assimilation will vary indefinitely. The assimilation—as the very term implies—will be conditioned, coloured and modified by the subject who assimilates. This is the subjective factor of all experience. *Quidquid recipitur, recipitur secundum modum recipientis.*

Nor, again, does religious experience involve any rejection or disparagement of external cultus, public worship, sacraments and ceremonies. On the contrary, just as it is normally accompanied by and requires a conceptual interpretation, it also tends to be associated with, and in fact demands for its full utilisation and fruitfulness, some exterior and sensible expression. This indeed is but to say that it is the experience of an embodied spirit.

Nor even would I maintain that our knowledge of God is confined to the data of religious experience and their interpretation. As we have already seen, metaphysical intuitions, not directly religious in quality, ontological, psychological, and cosmological, separately and in combination establish or display, 'monstrate' the existence of a super-personal God, the transcendent and distinct first Cause of the universe. And although in the concrete the consideration of these metaphysical intuitions and their implications is apt to be accompanied by a distinctively religious apprehension of the Divine Object to which they relate, they are always separable theoretically and sometimes even in practice. But a metaphysical theism devoid of religious experience is merely formal, intellectually sufficient to produce conviction, but woefully inadequate to satisfy the needs of the spirit. For the knowledge of God thus obtained is notional, not real; abstract, not concrete; dead, not living; a practical, if not also a theoretical, deism.

Religious experience is thus the soul of religion, without which it is a corpse. But the soul in turn cannot function apart from its body, conceptual interpretation and sensible cultus.

The better to understand the relation between religious experience in the raw and its conceptual interpretation we will consider Pascal's famous conversion experience, as recorded in the Memorial he wore on his person till death:

FIRE

God of Abraham, God of Isaac, God of Jacob,
Not of philosophers or men of learning.
Certainty, joy, certainty, feeling, sight, joy,
God of Jesus Christ.
My God and your God.
Thy God shall be my God.   Ruth.
Oblivion of the world and all outside God.
Joy, Joy, tears of Joy.

Fire.—Here we have the raw experience with only that minimum of interpretation necessary to utter it at all. Then, almost as close to the actual experience, its expression by a statement of its psychological effects: certainty, joy, tears of joy, feeling, sight, oblivion of all besides. Then, a further degree removed—My God and your God—The God of the Patriarchs, Ruth, Jesus Christ, not of philosophers and learned men. This is more mixed. It expresses a direct intuition of an Absolute Being, with whom the subject has entered into an intimate personal relation—an Absolute, therefore, more, not less, than personal. And this concrete living experience of a Personal God stands out in vivid contrast with the notional theism which is the utmost philosophers or savants can attain without distinctively religious experience. This interpretation would hardly have been formulated so explicitly if Pascal had not al-already accepted the Christian doctrine of God. It is not, however, read into the experience; the exper-ience, regarded in the light of previous knowledge, is seen to contain it. It is implicit in the experience. On the other hand, the historical statements that the God thus revealed is the God known by the Patri-archs and Jesus, were not contained in the experience. Nor indeed was the statement, though presumably the direct negative experience of Pascal himself that philosophy and learning cannot apprehend Him in this way. Conceptual interpretation is wedded from the first with the direct religious experience otherwise unutterable and sterile.

Moreover an external embodiment of the experi-ence is represented by the composition and wearing of the Memorial, and more widely by Pascal's devout Catholic observance.

Religious experience is thus a relative experience of the Absolute, not a pure Absolute. And this is, of course, true of religion generally. It is a mistake to call Catholicism, as Wust calls it,[5] the *absolute* religion. The only absolute religion conceivable is the beatific vision of God as He is, and even this is not in the strictest sense the absolute religion, for the vision of one saint is not identical in measure or quality with that of another. The vision of God enjoyed by each is unique, though the object is the same. Strictly speaking God's self-knowledge is the sole absolute religion. Still less is an absolute religion possible on earth, though all religion contains as such an absolute factor, being a communication of the Absolute to man. On the other hand, all forms of religion are not equally true. In their measure of truth and value they vary indefinitely, and, as Baron von Hügel has pointed out in this connection, in the sphere of religion every additional truth or value is of 'profound importance.'[6]

God nowhere leaves Himself without witness, but reveals Himself to souls, even through the crudest and most inadequate vehicles. Indeed we can often detect that Divine communication behind and despite conceptual interpretations which distort and obscure, sometimes even deny, its content. Richard

[5] *The Catharsis of the Creative Genius.*
[6] *Essays and Addresses on the Philosophy of Religion,* First Series, p. 269.

Jefferies, for example, victim of nineteenth-century scepticism, rejects intellectually a theism which his experience forces into the very terminology of the Areopagite. And Mr. Middleton Murry is granted an experience of transcendent Godhead of overwhelming cogency, in such conflict with his naturalistic prejudice that he violently explains it away by an immanental interpretation which glaringly contradicts his own account of the experience thus 'disinfected' of its content.[7] But the experience bears its testimony the more powerfully for these attempted suppressions of its witness.

On the other hand, the great historic revelation begun by the Patriarchs and lawgivers of Judaism, continued by its prophets and culminating in Jesus and the Church He founded, interprets, secures, fertilises and harmonises the broken lights of religious truth received and registered in 'diverse portions and manners,' πολυμερῶς καὶ πολυτρόπως, by the religious experience of mankind in every age and place, with a completeness and adequacy not to be found elsewhere, though still infinitely inadequate to the Absolute Divine Reality. The value of the *Summa* is not destroyed by the fact that its author found

---

[7] Christopher Dawson, *Christianity and the New Age,* in *Essays in Order,* pp. 192ff.

himself unable to complete it, after a high experience of God—which yet was not the beatific vision.

Nevertheless, earnest seekers after religious truth grope with lanterns in full daylight, searching the ends of the earth for fragments of Oriental wisdom, Hindu, Buddhist, or Taoist, partial, confused, and ill-understood, though a religion which comprehends, exceeds, interprets and co-ordinates these scattered gleams awaits them all the while at home, the Christianity which they reject because they do not know it and imagine that they do. A superficial acquaintance with the exterior of Christian doctrine, even perhaps in its complete Catholic statement, is the veil which conceals its inner riches. They see only what a child sees and miss the treasure of profound and comprehensive wisdom that lies beyond. If instead of seeking truth in Eastern scriptures, whose meaning even on points of fundamental importance is disputed by learned Orientalists, they would but study the great Catholic theologians and mystics, Augustine and Bernard, Bonaventure and Thomas, Ruysbroeck and Tauler, Teresa and John of the Cross,[8] they might realise the futility of searching strange creeds for morsels of the banquet spread close at hand, which

---

[8] I say nothing of the New Testament, as it has probably been misread into insignificance.

alone can satisfy their spiritual hunger, and from
which in ignorance they have turned away.

Direct religious experience, as we should expect,
varies indefinitely in value and quality. At its lowest
it is little more than a religious colouring of purely
immanental intuition, a nature-mysticism, as much
artistic as religious, and the genuine transcendental
experience, experience, that is to say, of a God other
than the soul or the universe, presents an entire
gamut of quality and degree from a vague sense of
divine presence which would pass unperceived if its
subject did not already possess some definite religious
belief, to the mystical experience of infused prayer.

Baron von Hügel, in this, as he tells us, a disciple
of 'Ideal' Ward, attempted to draw an ethical frontier between nature and supernature. He would have
us regard all heroic self-sacrifice as supernatural.[9]
This I can only consider a serious mistake. The
anarchist Bakunin, and the Communist leader Lenin
displayed heroic self-devotion. But it would surely
be absurd to find the supernatural at work in the
direction of movements fundamentally and vehe-
mently opposed to the supernatural. Not even martyr-
dom need be supernatural, if endured for some purely

    [9] *Essays and Addresses on the Philosophy of Religion*, First
Series, p. 280; cf. also pp. 224, 285, 287.

humanitarian cause without reference to God. The criterion of the supernatural of which we are in search will not be ethical, but distinctly religious. Religious values are more incommensurable with ethical than the stellar universe with the surface of the earth. They belong to a wholly different order. May we not say that wherever we have transcendent religion, even if the transcendent reference be inadequately expressed or even if it be actually denied by the interpretation placed upon it, supernatural grace is operative, whether actual or habitual? Is it not legitimate, indeed required by the evidence, to extend St. Paul's criterion, 'No man can say Jesus is Lord but by the Holy Ghost,' to all experience—whether explicitly formulated as such or not—of God as the transcendent and Absolute Lord of a creation wholly distinct from His Godhead, who enters into a personal relation with the soul because He is Himself more, not less, than personal? This is, not to say that God as the object of religious experience is solely apprehended as transcendent. His intimate presence in the soul and His infinite attraction as the fulness of value and the fulfilment of desire are also apprehended, at times more powerfully. Apprehended as immanent in His intimate union and attraction, God is experienced as what Professor

Otto [10] has called *mysterium fascinosum,* the fasci-
nating mystery. Apprehended as transcendence and
otherness, He is experienced as *mysterium tremendum,* the awful mystery or majesty.[11] These complementary aspects, which correspond respectively to the
unitive and the contemplative modes of human apprehension of which now one, now the other predominates in religious experience, even to the temporary exclusion of its complement from the field of
consciousness, represent the love and awe which are
combined in man's religious attitude to God.

In two most important articles published in the
Révue d'Ascêtique et de Mystique by Père Picard,
S.J., under the title *La Saisie immédiate de Dieu,*[12]
the author argues that the human soul possesses of
its very nature an obscure apprehension of God. It is
so obscure that it cannot even distinguish its Divine
Object. He is touched like an object in the dark, an
unknown something. With the advent of grace this
contact becomes what the writer calls *'clair confus,'*
'clear but confused,' a presence and plenitude in the
background of the spirit and its activities, clear in the
sense that it is recognised as Divine, but otherwise
still obscure. Even in mystical prayer the obscurity

[10] *The Idea of the Holy* (Das Heilige), ch. 4.
[11] *Ibid.,* ch. 7.
[12] Since republished in book form.

remains—there can be no distinct vision in this life—
but God is now experienced, no longer as simply
present but as acting upon the soul, who feels herself
the passive recipient of His operation within her.
Both these higher forms of intuition are religious experience. Objectively indeed even the first is religious experience, but the subject is not conscious of
its nature.

Religious experience, however, is not only concerned with God in Himself; it extends to His operations in creatures, and their relations to Him. The
Communion of Saints in God may also be experienced by the soul, obscurely for the most part, but
with a conviction more powerful than could be produced by mere reflection on a doctrine accepted only
externally. Electricity, in itself invisible and in-
tangible, becomes visible in the lamps it lights,
sensible in the power it supplies. So God becomes,
as it were, visible in the Saints, who shine with the
supernatural splendour of the Word, tangible in the
works of supernatural charity, which the Spirit in-
spires them to accomplish. The connecting cables
are the channels of grace, visible and invisible.
God's social revelation is the Communion of Saints,
the mystical Christ, the extension in time and space
of the historic. The relation between this Commu-

nion of Saints in God, God present revealed and operative in this mystical society, and the visible Church corresponds with the relation between religious experience and concrete religious practice in the individual. In both cases the former is the soul of the latter. The Church exists to embody and serve on earth the Communion of Saints, as external religious practice exists to embody and serve that union of God with the soul which in one form or another constitutes religious experience. That the Church is not coterminous with the Communion of Saints on earth, that religious practice may exist without the corresponding religious experience or the latter without adequate exterior embodiment, are imperfections, clamorous for their removal.

If the *raison d'être* of the Church is thus to express and mediate God's self-revelation and self-communication in the society of souls supernaturally united with Himself, to join or support the Church for some other reason, for instance, as a principle of social, political, economic, ethical, or intellectual order, is to misconstrue her essence and purpose. And it is peculiarly fatal to fly to the Church as a refuge of despair, not for the positive religious value she conveys, but as a haven from some particular evil, real or imaginary, outside her pale, because the need is felt for some definite code of belief and conduct, and therefore the truth of Catholic doctrine is to be pragmatically assumed, or even because a man must have some voluntary allegiance, and nothing better presents itself. This is to behave towards the Bride of God and Mother of Saints like the child of Belloc's *Cautionary Tales,* who was bidden 'always to keep hold of nurse, for fear of finding something worse.' Such is the disaster and degradation of seeking a religious institution for anything except religion—for loaves and fishes, social, intellectual or ethical; which, if more spiritual than bodily food, are no better able to satisfy man's hunger for God.

Baron von Hügel distinguished three elements in religion, the mystical—the term is here used too loosely to denote all direct religious experience—the rational, and the institutional. He was right in insisting that these three factors are necessarily present in all religion that is healthy and adequate to human needs. But the rational and institutional elements are not essentially or in themselves religious. Religion is in its essence wholly and solely the mystical or more correctly the experimental element.[13] The other two elements become religious

[13] Baron von Hügel uses both terms as though they were synonymous. This initial confusion obscures his entire treatment of mysticism.

only when associated with the former. The rational
is its conceptual interpretation, the institutional its
external and material embodiment. They are related
to the 'mystical', the experimental element, as the
discursive reason and the body are related to the
spirit. When the spirit leaves the body discursive
reason ceases, and the body, strictly a body no
longer, is doomed to corruption. Similarly when
religious experience—personal and experimental
religion—is absent, there is nothing to be conceptu-
ally interpreted. The record of past interpretation
indeed remains as the writings of a dead man remain.
And this scripture becomes spiritually alive whenever it is again brought into contact with living
religion. Till then it is a dead letter. And institutional religion is a corpse, corrupting and poisonous
until it is buried out of sight. And if this spiritual
death, however common in individuals, or even
groups, never befalls the Church as a whole, it is
because the living presence of God, her Soul, never
leaves His Body, but is always operative and sensible in the vital religion of her living members.
This vital union with God, living religion, is holiness. The Divine Holiness is the ultimate religious
category or quality apprehended in religious experience, God apprehended in His transcendent dis-

tinction from creatures.[14] And the vital communication and presence of that holiness is the holiness of creatures. The Church lives because she is Holy, the corporate tabernacle of the Holy God where He dwells amongst men and reveals Himself to them. The objective Holiness of Doctrine and Sacrament, itself due to the living Holiness of God present in both, is only realised as an active force in human life when it is vitally apprehended and assimilated as living and personal religious experience. To think or act otherwise, subordinating the experimental element of religion, in short, religion, to its conceptual and institutional embodiments is doctrinal and ecclesiastical materialism. The primary and intrinsic holiness of the Church does not consist in the fact that 'she teaches a holy doctrine and offers to all the means of holiness'—this is but the double embodiment, conceptual and institutional of her true holiness—but in the abiding Presence of the Holy Spirit manifest in 'the eminent holiness of so many of her children.' *Omnis gloria filæ regis ab intus.*

[14] Otto, *The Idea of the Holy* (Das Heilige), passim.

MYSTICISM

SINCE every level of being is the reflection of a higher and all in their degree reflections of Absolute Being, we have always found ourselves, when considering some lower manifestation of God, brought almost insensibly to His supreme manifestation in religious experience, and often even to the highest form of that experience, namely, mystical union. For mysticism is no extrinsic or accidental ornament of religion, a miraculous or quasi-miraculous gift like prophecy, healing or special revelation. It is organically connected with the normal supernatural life of sanctifying grace. If glory, the beatific vision of God, be the flower of grace—'grace at home' as Faber has aptly expressed it—mystical prayer is its bud. It is supernatural life become self-conscious, the intuition of God present and active in the soul by grace. Sanctifying grace is a reception of God's own life in the soul. That is why it is essentially *supernatural*. As received in the powers of the soul this life is faith, the reception of God's self-knowledge by the understanding, and charity, the reception of His self-love by the will. And as in the Blessed Trinity the Word and the Holy Spirit proceed from the Father,[1] so the reception of God's self-knowledge and love in the understanding and will proceed from His presence in the ground of both, that centre of the soul which the mystics call, by diverse metaphors, its apex or summit and fundus or depth. Thus, if the entire creation is an external continuation of the interior life of the Trinity, this is pre-eminently and most strictly true of the supernatural life of the soul. Normally the supernatural reception of God's life and operations is sub-conscious. God, as Père Picard points out, is not apprehended as active in the soul, the source of her supernatural acts. If He is apprehended obscurely as present by grace, He is not apprehended as the active source of spiritual life. Indeed the acts of the soul are still mostly natural, at best subordinate to a radical orientation of supernatural love. In the majority of souls, the supernatural life is a seed buried in the subconscious, or, if more, a shoot not perceptibly very different from their natural life. In its earlier growth there is noth-

---

[1] The Spirit also proceeds from the Son. The love of God presupposes an apprehension of God however obscure. But only in heaven does the union of love proceed from a clear perception of God by the understanding. In the obscurity of this life the union of the will is primary.

ing or very little to distinguish a wild from a culti-
vated variety of the same plant, a weed from a flower
of similar foliage and habit. As, however, the supernatural life grows in the soul and progressively com-
mands and informs her natural activities, the soul
becomes conscious of that life within herself. To
her closer union with God corresponds an intuition
of that union, therefore of His supernatural presence
and activity. And in so far as the soul's life and
action are now a reception of God's, the union and
its intuition are predominantly passive: not inactivity
but the more intense passive-activity of receiving
God, the Pure Act.

It is no objection to this organic view of mysticism
that souls without mystical experience are often
holier than those who enjoy it, and that among their
number there may even be canonised saints. Different liquids do not boil at the same temperature. An
equal measure of light does not penetrate equally
an opaque and a transparent substance. Souls whose
natural disposition, or psycho-physical temperament,
is opaque to spiritual light will not become conscious
of their supernatural union with God, when it has
attained a degree at which it becomes perceptible to
more transparent subjects. Mystical union must correspond accurately with the degree of supernatural

love in the will, for it is effected by that love. The factor which makes the mystical union mystical experience, namely, the intuition of that union, will depend in part on subjective natural conditions, physiological and temperamental—even on the attitude towards mysticism of the subject and his environment. The saint is necessarily a mystic in fact, if not necessarily in experience. Mystical experience, however, is the normal concomitant of mystical union.

Moreover the will penetrates deeper than the understanding into the centre or apex of the soul, which is pre-eminently the seat of God's presence. It is for that reason that the mystics term the centre the apex of the will, and that the will is the principal instrument or rather vehicle of the mystical union with God. To every degree of ascent on the ladder of being corresponds subjectively a deeper psychological function, which apprehends the higher level and is united with it. The soul is therefore united with God through her profoundest function, or more truly the profound root of all her functions, namely, the centre. So profound indeed is this ultimate centre that it has been mistaken for another self, greater and wider than the normal ego. This error, though seemingly countenanced by certain aspects of mys-

tical experience, contradicts that essential unity of
the individual person to which our experience as a
whole bears ample witness. Far from being another
self, or spirit distinct from the soul, the centre is the
root and unification of all the lower psychological
functions, the essential ego where the individual is
most himself, though at the same time most open to
God. And it is as the root of the will that the centre
chiefly manifests itself, the radical self, where the
self in its inmost selfhood is united with God by the
supernatural bond of charity.

If mystical experience is thus the organic unfolding and earthly fulfilment of the supernatural life—
if it is indeed, as we have seen, pre-eminently the
communication to creatures of the life of God in His
Trinity—it is most deplorable that mysticism should
still be so widely regarded with suspicion even by
Catholic writers, as something abnormal, even rather
queer, something with which the healthy religion of
normal folk has and should have no concern. Or at
best it is considered an extraordinary favour, granted
like miracle-working to a few chosen souls, with
which the ordinary Catholic has nothing whatever to
do. Yet mysticism is the very life-blood of sanctity.
Many see in mysticism only the joy and sweetness

which, except in certain negative stages, the intuition-union normally occasions, but which no more constitute the union or even the intuition which they accompany than the pleasure which normally accompanies the perception of beauty is that perception itself. Many also, despite the express warnings of mystical writers, still confuse mystical experience with those accidental concomitants, visions and voices, which are the translation of his intuition by the subconscious art of a mystic endowed with the requisite psycho-physical temperament into visual or verbal imagery, as the artist consciously translates his intuitions into pictorial images or into verbal or musical symbols. Others fail to distinguish in ecstasy, the state of anæsthesia due to the weakness of the human body from the mystical union and intuition which overcome its powers, and which alone is of value. And there runs as an undertone through this depreciation of mysticism the widespread prejudice against passionate religion, a belated and illogical survival of the Victorian horror of 'the passionate nature of art, love, and Roman Catholic Religion.' [2] These prejudices once removed, and the necessary discriminations made, mysticism may surely

[2] Shaw, *You Never Can Tell,* Act I., stage directions. The phrase is omitted in the omnibus edition, where the directions have been surreptitiously recast.

be recognised by all who accept the objective truth of religion for what it is, religion in its highest, purest and most intense form, the culmination of that religious experience which we have found to be the soul of religion, indeed in the strict sense religion itself.

If this be so, why, it may be asked, have we considered mystical experience apart under the symbolism of the rays beyond red? The answer is contained in what we have just said. As the visible red passes into the invisible, experienced only in its effects, so the knowledge of God expressed by conceptual theology or sensible imagery passes into the mystical apprehension beyond concept or image. It corresponds at one end of the scale of human experience to the experience of that primal 'matter-energy'—of whose nature science can tell us nothing, though its agency is being harnessed to our purposes—which we have symbolised by the ultra-violet at the other end of the spectrum. Of God, the Absolute Fulness of Being, and of matter, its minimum, we know only *that* they are, not *what* they are. And the mystical intuition which knows God most fully knows best that He is beyond knowledge. Only the seeming denials of the negative theology can utter what is here experienced. Yet these negations deny only limits upon a Being too positive for our essentially limited

categories, the perfect Determination which transcends our determinations with their inevitable factor
of negation.[8]

This Divine Unintelligibility, the Absolute Intelligibility of Perfect Being, is thus the opposite pole
to the unintelligibility of matter-energy, which is due
to its defect of being, its indetermination. In this
sanctuary unprofaned by concept or image 'praise is
silent in Zion,'[4] and prayer 'a union of nothing with
Nothing.'[5] When therefore the soul is asked to give
an account of what has passed within her she cannot
tell. The ecstatic delights of which the mystics are
so eloquent are but the overflow into the inferior
powers of the soul, sometimes even into the body, of
that central silence, 'the dark silence wherein all
lovers lose themselves.' [6] The joy of the union there
effected, 'the operation of silence,' so intense that
Blessed Angela of Foligno would not barter from it
'the space of an eye-wink' for all the joys, bodily or
spiritual, profane or sacred in the world besides, is
beyond expression, not to be imagined or conceived.[7]

[8] See Wust's criticism of Spinoza's axiom, *omnis determinatio
est negatio. Die Dialektik des Geistes,* pp. 89, *seq.*
[4] The literal rendering of *Psalm* lxiv., 1 (R. V. lxv., 1, margin).
[5] Father Augustine Baker, *Sancta Sophia,* Section IV., Ch. 6;
ed. 1911, p. 545.
[6] Ruysbroeck, *Adornment of the Spiritual Marriage,* iii, 4 (Trs.
Wynschenk Dom).
[7] *Book of Angela of Foligno.* Ed. Père Doncœur, S.J., Chap.
IX., pp. 91 and 93.

This supreme union and its delights are indeed, like the vision and joy of Heaven of which they are pledge and foretaste, the indescribable reward of God's lovers, *'merces magna nimis,'* 'which eye hath not seen nor ear heard, neither hath it entered into the heart of man.'

Since on earth there is no open vision, the mode of direct union here exceeds the mode of adoring contemplation. More correctly we should speak of aspects rather than modes, for in this supreme union with God contemplation and contact are substantially one. Indeed there are moments when the contact with God is so close and the reception of God so complete that the soul loses sight of its distinct selfhood, and is no longer self-conscious, but solely God-conscious. But because the soul is nevertheless distinct from God—a creature, not the Creator—self-consciousness returns, and in Heaven will no doubt subsist in and through the God-consciousness. But these are words, and we have reached the silence beyond. At the rainbow's end, the invisible ray of supreme union, the utmost self-communication of Divine Love, is lost in the unrefracted whiteness of Absolute Being. Thought fails in adoration and adoration is dumb.

CONCLUSION

WE have looked at every band of God's bow, have climbed in thought the ladder of human experience, and with it the degrees of objective being, from the lowest to the highest rung. And this by the double ascent of concrete union and abstract speculation, till in the highest form of experience both met as aspects of the same union. Everywhere we have found God present and active, though in unequal measure. Everywhere all positive being proved His reflection and communication, all positive agency His act. Only defect of beings belongs solely to the creature— particularly the privation which hinders the fulfilment of its specific nature, a privation the more fatal the higher in rank the nature to which it attaches. Everywhere this shadow of defect and evil follows created being, and the shadows are darkest where the sun shines brightest. Every advance involves a retreat, every gain a loss, and the most valuable things are worst abused. But if this shadow of evil denies a too facile optimism, no justification has appeared for a radical pessimism. On the contrary, evil is

everywhere secondary to good, and therefore less
powerful, and as creation ascends the scale of being
the light gains on the darkness. We have seen God's
blessed life of self-knowledge and self-love in His
Trinity in Unity continued in creatures and communicated to them—by reflection and analogy in the order
of nature, immediately and substantially in the order
of grace. If we have learnt not to make our home
among the natural images of the Divine Truth,
Goodness and Beauty, we can use and enjoy them for
what they are. We can take our delight in watching
the inter-play, so inexhaustibly rich and various, of
these lights reflected from the Divine Beauty upon
the abyss of nothingness. It is the copy of that eternal play of the ideas, their exemplars in the Wisdom
of God, *ludens coram eo omni tempore*. What is
strictly true of the soul supernaturally united with
God, and of the society of these souls whose visible
organ is the Church, is true in its measure of creation
as a whole. 'All the glory of the King's daughter is
from within,' from the Divine Word, from Whom
all her forms proceed and in Whom they subsist.
And therefore 'her clothing', the outer world which
our senses perceive, 'is of woven gold wrought with
embroidered colours.' In this contemplation 'all
things are ours' if we are God's, and we are certain

that 'all things,' however irrational or evil, 'work together' willy-nilly to the good of those who love Him. If at so many points the pattern of God's design in creation is lost in darkness, we know what are its guiding lines and that they will be completed. The positive doctrine of pantheism, that God is present and active in all that exists and acts, is accepted and justified by this view of the universe. We reject only its doctrine—logically implied, when not explicitly admitted—that the deficiency and evil of creatures is in and from God, and that all things participate and reflect Him in equal measure, so that cancer and hate are as divine as health and love. The view of human experience as God's rainbow unites a fundamental optimism with due regard to the facts of evil and suffering, idealism with realism, comprehension with distinction, attachment with detachment. It is historic without being historicist, absolute yet relative, broad without being shallow, profound without being narrow, religious without being fanatical, contemplative but inspiring action in every sphere; it is individualist, because the individual is a unique communication and image of God, yet social, because only a community of spirits can reflect His multiplicity in unity; it renounces the world as end, to accept it as means; the spirit 'is hid with Christ in

God,' but the feet are firmly planted on earth; it combines the patience born of the contemplation of eternity with the activity which responds to the unique opportunity of the passing moment; if it is theocentric, it is also humanist, for it sees in man God's likeness and temple; it is spiritual, yet values the body in which spirit is incarnate, the material in which its ideas are forms of visible loveliness; its glance pierces to the darkness of matter below, sweeps through all the ranks and provinces of created being, biological and spiritual, and rises to be lost once more in the light of Godhead. In a word it is Catholic.

ESSAYS IN ORDER

GENERAL EDITORS
Christopher Dawson & T. F. Burns

No. 1. *RELIGION AND CULTURE*
By Jacques Maritain. With a General Introduction to Essays in Order by Christopher Dawson.

No. 2. *CRISIS IN THE WEST*
By Peter Wust. With an Introduction by E. I. Watkin.

No. 3. *CHRISTIANITY AND THE NEW AGE*
By Christopher Dawson

No. 4. *THE BOW IN THE CLOUDS*
By E. I. Watkin

No. 5. *THE NECESSITY OF POLITICS*
By Carl Schmitt. With an Introduction by Christopher Dawson.

No. 6. *THE RUSSIAN REVOLUTION*
By Nicholas Berdyaev

No. 7. *THE DRIFT OF DEMOCRACY*
By M. de la Bedoyère

174

CANISIUS COLLEGE LIBRARY
BT135 .W28 1932
The bow in the cloud

3 5084 00115 8214